Grammar, Usage, and Mechanics Book

McDougal Littell

GRADE TWELVE

Teaching

More Practice

Application

 McDougal Littell
A HOUGHTON MIFFLIN COMPANY
Evanston, Illinois Boston Dallas

ISBN 0-618-30395-2

7 8 9 – CKI – 07 06

Contents

Special Features

The *Grammar, Usage, and Mechanics Workbook* contains a wealth of skill-building exercises.

Each lesson has different levels of worksheets. **Teaching** introduces the skill; **More Practice** and **Application** extend the skill with advanced exercises.

Worksheets correspond to lessons in the Pupil's Edition.

Each page focuses on one topic or skill. A brief instructional summary on the **Teaching** page is followed by reinforcement activities.

Key words and phrases are highlighted for greater clarity and ease of use.

When appropriate, example sentences demonstrate how to complete exercises.

Name _____ Date _____

Lesson 1 — Kinds of Clauses

Teaching

A **clause** is a group of words that contains both a subject and a verb. An **independent clause** expresses a complete thought and can stand alone as a sentence.

The South American rain forests support a diversity of life forms.
SUBJECT   VERB

A **subordinate clause,** or **dependent clause,** contains a subject and a verb but does not express a complete thought and cannot stand alone as a sentence.

When the wind erodes mountains (What happens at this time?)
SUBJECT   VERB

A subordinate clause must always be combined with an independent clause.

When the wind erodes mountains, flat-topped mesas and plateaus are created.
SUBORDINATE CLAUSE   INDEPENDENT CLAUSE

Two kinds of words that link or introduce clauses are coordinating conjunctions and subordinating conjunctions. A **coordinating conjunction** joins two independent clauses. Examples of coordinating conjunctions are *and, or, but*, and *yet*.

The Pacific Ocean is the largest ocean, and Mt. Everest is the highest mountain.
COORDINATING
CONJUNCTION

A **subordinating conjunction** introduces a subordinate clause.

Because deserts receive only a little rainfall, they are often covered by sand.
SUBORDINATING
CONJUNCTION

The following are some examples of subordinating conjunctions: *after, although, as, because, before, if, in order that, provided, since, so that, until, when, where, wherever, while.*

Identifying Kinds of Clauses and Conjunctions

In each sentence, identify the boldfaced group of words by writing **IND** for an independent clause and **SUB** for a subordinate clause. Then find the conjunction in the sentence. Underline a coordinating conjunction once and a subordinating conjunction twice.

1. Although the oceans appear to be separated, **they are actually joined together.** _____

2. **Before echo sounding was developed,** the depth of the ocean was measured with weighted lines of hemp or wire. _____

3. The ocean's currents are studied in detail **because they are important to shipping.** _____

4. Whenever Earth's plates slide past one another, **earthquakes can occur.** _____

5. **The North Pole is covered by water,** and the South Pole is covered by land. _____

6. Erupting volcanoes cause great destruction, yet **they also bring many benefits.** _____

7. **As coastal areas become flooded,** the need for wetlands becomes clear. _____

Tabs make it easy to navigate the book.

CHAPTER 3

Review 1

Nouns

Teaching

A **noun** is a word that names a person, place, thing, or idea.

Type of Noun	Definition	Example
common noun	general name for a person, place, thing, or idea	architect
proper noun	name of a particular person, place, thing, or idea	Frank Lloyd Wright
singular noun	one person, place, thing, or idea	building
plural noun	more than one person, place, thing, or idea	buildings
collective noun	name of a group regarded as a unit	crew
concrete noun	name of something perceptible to the senses	brick
abstract noun	name of something the senses cannot perceive	beauty
compound noun	two or more words used together as one noun	saltbox
possessive noun	a noun that shows ownership	artist's vision, artists' visions

Finding Nouns

Underline every noun in each sentence.

1. When you see an attractive building, thank the architect who designed it.

2. Architects design buildings both to provide shelter and to create beauty.

3. Architects also design monuments dedicated to the memory of important people and events.

4. The beauty of a city is determined by the quality of its architecture.

5. Architecture dates from prehistoric times and is found in almost all societies.

6. A society's architecture reflects the values of its people.

7. Unique styles of architecture have developed in the various cultures of the world.

8. In America, the first architecture copied Europe's styles.

9. In the Southwest, missionaries built churches of adobe that combined the styles of Spain and the American Indians.

10. In the northern colonies, the settlers built homes of wood with sloping roofs.

11. In the southern colonies, planters constructed large residences that were similar to England's country estates.

12. The Industrial Revolution created a demand for new types of buildings.

13. For centuries, architects had planned religious buildings, castles, and houses.

14. With the growth of industrialization, architects needed to design structures such as factories, warehouses, and offices.

15. When they decided not to copy the styles of other countries, America's architects started to make an impact on the world's architecture.

16. The skyscraper, the best-known symbol of modern architecture, was developed in the United States.

17. Chicago became the center of modern architecture in the United States as the city rebuilt after the Great Chicago Fire.

18. Recently, people have developed a concern for the preservation of old buildings with architectural value.

Nouns

More Practice

REVIEW

A. Identifying Nouns

Identify each numbered and italicized noun by writing **common, proper, abstract, concrete, collective, compound,** or **possessive** on the corresponding line below. Each noun belongs to at least two categories.

Frank Lloyd Wright was one of **(1)** *America's* most distinguished architects. Wright was an advocate of functional architecture; that is, he believed that every part of a building should express its **(2)** *use*. Nothing unnecessary should be added. His works ranged from private homes to public **(3)** *museums*. He even made plans for a **(4)** *skyscraper* one mile high. He designed the **(5)** *Imperial Hotel* in Tokyo. It was one of the few buildings to survive undamaged after a severe earthquake struck the city in 1923.

In 1932, Wright founded the Taliesin Fellowship. The fellowship was a **(6)** *group* of architectural students who paid to live and work with Wright. During the 1930s, **(7)** *Wright's* projects included the *Falling Water House,* a private house dramatically perched over a **(8)** *waterfall*. It is a sensational house with glass everywhere to bring **(9)** *Mother Nature* into the living room. Wright's daring designs and complex use of geometric shapes have inspired a whole **(10)** *community* of architects.

1. _____   6. _____

2. _____   7. _____

3. _____   8. _____

4. _____   9. _____

5. _____   10. _____

B. Identifying Nouns

Underline the noun or nouns described in parentheses after each sentence.

1. Architects in Egypt often built monuments to their kings, both living and dead. (proper noun)

2. Egyptians built tombs for their rulers in pyramids, four-sided buildings with pointed tops. (common noun)

3. Pyramids were not the only buildings that ancient architects designed, however. (concrete noun)

4. The temple of Queen Hatshepsut built around 1480 B.C. is considered to be a masterpiece of ancient architecture. (compound noun)

5. In honor of her, the Queen's subjects erected it at the foot of a massive cliff, joining nature and architecture. (possessive noun)

6. It is easy to imagine gangs of workers struggling to move huge rocks into place. (collective noun)

7. The beauty and mystery of ancient pyramids and temples continue to fascinate people. (abstract noun)

Review 1 # Nouns

A. Supplying Nouns

Complete the paragraph by supplying nouns as indicated in parentheses. Write each word you would use on the blank line.

> One of my favorite buildings is the *(1. proper noun)*. The elements that I feel are most attractive in this building are its *(2. common nouns)*. In addition, the *(3. compound nouns)* are both functional and artistically effective. The architect used these materials: *(4. concrete noun)*, on the outside walls and *(5. concrete noun)* on the inside of the building. In my opinion, the *(6. possessive noun)* design works well. The *(7. collective noun)* that uses the building regularly should take time to admire its *(8. abstract noun)*.

1. _____   5. _____

2. _____   6. _____

3. _____   7. _____

4. _____

B. Writing with Nouns

Write sentences that contain the kinds of nouns indicated. Underline these nouns in your sentences.

1. Use a proper noun and a plural noun.

   _____

2. Use a common noun and a collective noun.

   _____

3. Use an abstract noun and a possessive noun.

   _____

4. Use a compound noun and a proper noun.

   _____

5. Use an abstract noun and a concrete noun.

   _____

6. Use a proper possessive noun and a concrete noun.

   _____

7. Use an abstract noun and a plural noun.

   _____

8. Use a concrete noun and a proper noun.

   _____

REVIEW

Pronouns

Teaching

A **pronoun** is a word used in place of a noun or another pronoun.

Type of Pronoun	Function	Examples
personal	refers to first person, second person, and third person	I, you, he
possessive	shows ownership or relationship	mine, ours
reflexive	reflects an action back on the subject	itself
intensive	emphasizes a noun or pronoun in the same sentence	yourself
interrogative	asks a question	who, what
demonstrative	points out specific persons, places, things, or ideas	that, those
relative	introduces a subordinate clause	who, what
indefinite	does not refer to a specific person or thing	all, each, several

Finding Pronouns

Underline all the pronouns in the following sentences.

1. A cartoon is a drawing or series of drawings that tells a story.
2. Each of the separate scenes in a cartoon is called a *panel*.
3. Most of the cartoonists do not draw people as they really appear.
4. These are artists who tend to exaggerate some of the features of a person.
5. For example, they may draw a person who has an oversized head.
6. Another of their techniques is to use symbols to help them tell a story.
7. They may use a light bulb above a character's head to indicate that the character is having an idea.
8. Most of us are familiar with comic strips, but what is an editorial cartoon?
9. An editorial cartoon is one of the most interesting kinds of cartoons you may see in a newspaper or magazine.
10. Editorial cartoons encourage their readers to develop an opinion about someone or something in the news.
11. Editorial cartoonists themselves have strong feelings about their topics.
12. Benjamin Franklin drew one of the first editorial cartoons urging all of the colonies to unite.
13. It showed each of the colonies as a part of a snake and had a caption that read, "Join or Die."
14. Thomas Nast made himself into a legend in cartooning when he introduced the elephant and donkey as symbols of the major political parties.
15. Comic strips are so popular that most of the newspapers in the country reserve one or more of their pages just for their comics.
16. In the early 1900s, a cartoonist whose name was Rube Goldberg drew cartoons that featured complicated contraptions.
17. The contraptions themselves were designed to accomplish simple tasks, but they were ridiculously complex.
18. None of Goldberg's readers would have used his inventions to do jobs that they could do more easily for themselves.

REVIEW

Review 2 **Pronouns**   *More Practice*

A. Finding Pronouns

Underline the pronoun or pronouns described in parentheses after each sentence.

1. I have never read either of these books. (indefinite)
2. Over the summer, he taught himself to juggle. (reflexive)
3. Who was the first one to read his report? (interrogative)
4. The candidates themselves proposed that they debate. (intensive)
5. Mr. Foster insisted that these were the tastiest cookies he had ever eaten. (demonstrative)
6. She is a principal whom everybody respects. (relative)
7. She asked if she could borrow our video camera. (possessive)
8. Our coach asked us to carry the equipment to his car. (personal)
9. I knocked on their door, and somebody answered. (indefinite)
10. Our teacher warned us that this was our last chance to order yearbooks. (demonstrative)
11. The author herself will be autographing her books at the mall. (intensive)
12. He proved to all of us and to himself that he could be a good leader. (reflexive)
13. Everyone agrees with me that this is the best restaurant in town. (relative)
14. Which of you left your umbrella in my car? (personal)
15. My parents always come to the games to watch me play. (possessive)

B. Identifying Pronouns

Complete each sentence with an appropriate pronoun. Then, on the line to the right, label the pronoun **personal, possessive, reflexive, intensive, interrogative, demonstrative, relative,** or **indefinite.**

1. _____ of the gymnasts had trained for years.   _____

2. _____ of the deities was the god of war?   _____

3. _____ are examples of early Roman sculpture.   _____

4. John Wilkes Booth, _____ was an actor, shot Abraham Lincoln.   _____

5. _____ of the formats is acceptable for the yearbooks.   _____

6. The official blew _____ whistle to stop the play.   _____

7. _____ is the scientific name for goldfish?   _____

8. When some people ride a roller coaster, _____ scream all the
   way down the first hill.   _____

9. Before you go to bed, calm _____ down with a glass of warm milk. _____

10. I was surprised when the senator _____ answered the phone.   _____

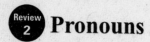

Pronouns

Application

A. Writing Sentences with Pronouns

Write sentences using the types of pronouns indicated. Underline the required pronouns in your sentences. Be sure the pronoun matches the person, number, and gender of its antecedent, when an antecedent is stated.

1. demonstrative pronoun

_____

2. possessive pronoun that stands alone

_____

3. personal pronoun in the first person

_____

4. personal pronoun in the third person

_____

_____

5. plural reflexive pronoun

_____

_____

B. Writing Dialogue with Pronouns

Underline all the pronouns in the dialogue below. Then write one more quotation for each of the two speakers. Include at least four of these kinds of pronouns: **personal, possessive, demonstrative, reflexive, intensive, interrogative, indefinite,** and **relative.** Underline the pronouns in your dialogue.

"Kallie, do you know where the newspaper comics are? I like to give myself a treat and read them every day."

"Alec, you are too old to be reading comics. No one over the age of ten reads them."

"You are wrong. Some of the comics make comments about what is going on in the world. Others provide insight into human relationships. Many are intended just to make us laugh. The comics are so important that when there was a newspaper strike in New York, the mayor himself, Fiorello La Guardia, read them to all of the people over the radio."

"I guess you have convinced me."

"So, what did you do with my comics?"

"I hid them so I could read them first."

_____

_____

_____

_____

_____

Review 3 # Verbs   *Teaching*

A **verb** is a word used to express an action, a condition, or a state of being.

An **action verb** expresses a physical or mental action. Action verbs may be transitive or intransitive. A **transitive verb** transfers the action from the subject toward a direct object. An **intransitive verb** does not transfer action, so it does not have an object.

> **Transitive verb**   The goalie <u>caught</u> the ball. (*Ball* is the direct object.)
>
> **Intransitive verb**   The crowd <u>cheered</u>.

A **linking verb** connects the subject with a word or words that identify or describe the subject. It can connect the subject with a predicate nominative or a predicate adjective. Some linking verbs are forms of *be*, such as *am, is, was,* and *were*. Others express a condition, such as *appear, become, feel, look, remain, seem, sound,* and *taste.*

> Sean <u>was</u> the manager. He <u>seemed</u> confident.

An **auxiliary verb,** also called a **helping verb,** helps the main verb express action or make a statement. Auxiliary verbs also help indicate voice, mood, or tense. A **verb phrase** is made up of a main verb and one or more helping verbs. Some common auxiliary verbs are *had, been, do, is, might, will, must, could, should,* and *would.*

> The forwards <u>are running</u> down the field. (The main verb is *running.*)

A. Identifying Verbs

Underline the verb or verb phrase in each sentence. In the space above each underlined word, write **A** if it is an action verb, **L** if it is a linking verb, or **AUX** if it is an auxiliary verb.

1. The game of lacrosse <u>is</u> popular in many countries.
2. Players <u>move</u> the ball with sticks with net pockets at one end.
3. They <u>score</u> goals in the other team's goal.
4. Only the goalies <u>may touch</u> the ball.
5. Lacrosse <u>was adapted</u> from a Canadian Indian game.
6. The game <u>was</u> originally a rough sport.

B. Identifying Transitive and Intransitive Verbs

Underline the verb or verb phrase in each sentence. On the line, write **T** for a transitive verb or **I** for an intransitive verb.

1. In the past, tennis players usually wore white shorts or dresses. **T**

2. Perhaps the color white represented gentility to the upper class players. **I**

3. Today the rules for tennis wear have changed. **I**

4. The development of the tennis shoe improved tennis wear. **T**

5. Today's tennis shoe is crafted with comfort and support in mind. **I**

Review 3 # Verbs

More Practice

A. Identifying Verbs

Underline each verb once. If the verb has a direct object or objects, underline the direct object(s) twice. In the space above each verb, write **T** for transitive or **I** for intransitive.

1. The mayor presented the key to our city to the famous opera star.
2. Newspaper critics often differ in their evaluations of TV, theater, music, and food.
3. Samuel Langhorne Clemens wrote under the pen name Mark Twain.
4. The galaxies in our universe are moving apart rapidly.
5. The constant drip of calcium carbonate from cave roofs eventually forms stalactites.
6. Large roadside billboards advertise products and services along some highways.
7. Young children need constant care and attention.
8. Our family has moved three times in the past decade.
9. A strategic plan increased the enterprise's chances of success.
10. The instructions for the VCR confuse my grandparents.

B. Using Verbs

Refer to the passage below to complete these items.

Sports medicine is a field that provides health care to athletes and other active people. Sports medicine minimizes the risk of injury, and it treats injuries that do occur. A team of experts work together in this field. They evaluate training techniques, diagnose injuries, and determine treatment. Many athletic teams have arranged for the services of a team physician. The team physician will provide medical attention for the players. The team's trainer often assists. With proper care, athletes may return to playing as quickly as possible. Sports medicine has improved the general health of athletes.

1. Find examples of two transitive verbs in the passage. On the lines below, write those verbs and the direct objects that receive their actions.

   Transitive verb 1: __minimize__   Direct object: __risk evaluate__

   Transitive verb 2: __provide__   Direct object: __attention__

2. Write three action verbs from the passage on the lines below.

   __treats__   __work__   __evaluate__

3. Write two verb phrases from the passage. Underline the auxiliary verbs in each phrase.

   __may return__   __have arranged__

4. Write the sentence from the passage that contains a linking verb. Underline the two words that are connected by the linking verb.

   __Sport medicine is a field that provides health care to athletes and other active people__

5. Find examples of two intransitive verbs in the passage. Write them on the lines below.

   __assists__   __work__

Review 3 **Verbs**   *Application*

A. Writing with Verbs That Can Be Either Transitive or Intransitive

Underline the verb in each sentence. Write **T** above it if it is transitive or **I** if it is intransitive. Then, if it is transitive, use it as an intransitive verb in a sentence of your own. If it is intransitive, use it as a transitive verb. Write your new sentence on the line. The new sentences can be about any topic. You may change the form or tense of the verb if you wish.

   EXAMPLE This batter often <u>hits</u> to left field. *This batter often hits home runs.*

1. Professional pitchers throw with speed and accuracy.

_____

2. Their pitches reach speeds of well over 90 miles per hour.

_____

3. The manager calls loudly to the pitcher.

_____

4. The batter waves confidently to the crowd.

_____

5. The pitcher shakes his head in response to the catcher's signal.

_____

6. The ball flies out of the ballpark.

_____

B. Proofreading

The writer of this paragraph was careless and omitted many verbs. Proofread the paragraph, looking for places where an action verb, a linking verb, or an auxiliary verb would improve the writing. Then insert this proofreading symbol ⌄ and write the verb you wish to add above it.

There a wide variety of exciting winter sports. Some are familiar worldwide, such as ice skating and skiing. However, some not as well known. One example bobsledding, which is a fast, dangerous sport. A group of Englishmen and Americans introduced the sport in 1890. Bobsledders down a steep, icy course in sleds.

Another less-known winter sport tobogganing. Tobogganing coasting on snow on long sleds. Toboggans very fast and may achieve a speed of 60 miles per hour. Native American hunters often toboggans to carry game over the snow.

Ringette is a team sport that similar to ice hockey. The game invented in Ontario, Canada. Ringette teams consist of six players, all on ice skates. The game played on an ice rink. Girls and young women in Canada and the northern United States enjoy this game. Next winter, you want to try one of these sports.

Adjectives and Adverbs

Teaching

Adjectives and adverbs are modifiers that describe other words in a sentence.
Adjectives modify noun or pronouns. They qualify or specify the meaning of the
nouns or pronouns they modify. Adjectives answer the following questions: *What
kind? Which one? How many? How much?*

<u>colorful</u> fish   <u>this</u> pond   <u>three</u> boats   <u>enough</u> time

Some special types of adjectives are the following:

- **articles:** *a, an,* and *the*
- **nouns used as adjectives:** <u>lake</u> breeze
- **proper adjectives:** <u>Canadian</u> border
- **predicate adjectives,** which follow linking verbs and modify the subject:
  Fishing is <u>enjoyable</u>.

Adverbs modify verbs, adjectives, or other adverbs. They answer the following
questions about the words they modify: how *(strongly, happily);* where *(down,
here);* when *(early, tomorrow);* and to what extent *(very, so).*

Finding Adjectives and Adverbs

Underline once all the adjectives in the following sentences, ignoring the articles.
Underline the adverbs twice.

1. Fish live almost anywhere you find water.
2. Some fish can survive only in saltwater environments; other fish can live only in
   fresh water.
3. Many saltwater fish live in water that is always warm.
4. The warmest ocean water is around coral reefs, and over a thousand species of
   fish with fantastic shapes and brilliant colors swarm there.
5. Although most fish prefer warm water, the Arctic fish choose to live in cold
   water.
6. The various kinds of fish differ greatly in almost every aspect.
7. One unusual fish is the four-eyed fish, which has two-part eyes.
8. This fish often swims just at the surface of the water, and the top half of each
   eye sees above.
9. The bottom half of each eye sees underwater.
10. A few species of fish will occasionally attack a human being.
11. Certain kinds of piranhas are bloodthirsty fish with extremely sharp teeth.
12. Other fish have poisonous spines that can instantly injure or even kill an
    unfortunate victim.
13. Fish live in amazingly diverse locations.
14. Many fish live in shallow, coastal waters.
15. Open-ocean fish live far out to sea and rarely swim close to the shore.
16. Those fish that live deep in the ocean include the most unusual animals in the
    entire world.

Adjectives and Adverbs

Review 4

More Practice

A. Identifying Adjectives

In each of the following sentences, underline the adjectives and place the words that they modify in parentheses. More than one adjective may modify a noun. Do not underline articles.

1. It took us four (weeks) to refinish the Victorian (table.)
2. The hero of a literary (epic) may be a seeker, rather than a valiant (warrior)
3. Alison seemed unusually (calm) after the accident yesterday.
4. Senator and Mr. Eden led the dancers in a Viennese (waltz.)
5. Naturalists observe cheetahs in some parts of central (Africa)
6. (Traffic) was so heavy that we had to take an alternate (route.)
7. The computer (monitor) was difficult to read from the wrong (angle.)
8. The last-place (team) appeared surprisingly (jubilant.)
9. Many (people) admire the skill and artistry of Navajo (weavers.)
10. In an amazingly short (time) the empty wood (house) burned to the ground.

B. Identifying Adverbs

Underline the word the boldfaced adverb modifies. If it is a verb, write **V;** an adjective, **ADJ;** or an adverb, **ADV.**

1. Surprisingly, a snake's teeth are **very** delicate and often break.   ADV

2. Beethoven wrote nine symphonies but **only** one opera.   ADJ

3. Which did you like **better,** the book or the movie?   ADJ

4. Average American working adults **probably** will move every five years.   ADV

5. Jon wrote the invitation **extremely** carefully on the parchment paper.   ADV

6. Mr. Nuevo will drop us **off** at the library on his way home.   ADV

7. Angel approached the day of the track meet **quite** confidently.   ADJ

8. The life expectancy of women in the United States today is **significantly** higher than it was during the 19th century.   ADV

9. Upon entering the bookstore, we saw Joe **inside.**   ADV

10. The lawyers who attended the conference at this hotel recommend it **highly.**   ADV

Review 4

Adjectives and Adverbs

Application

A. Writing Sentences with Adjectives and Adverbs

Revise each of these plain sentences by adding at least one adjective and one adverb. You may also add phrases if you wish. Write your new sentence on the line. Underline the adjectives once and the adverbs twice.

EXAMPLE Fish swam in the aquarium.
Colorful fish swim *slowly* in the aquarium.

1. The mouths of the fish open and close.

   The small mouths of the fish open; close rapidly.

2. Their owner sprinkles food for them to eat.

   Their loving owner quickly skilled flakey food to them soon

3. The fish swim toward the food.

   The larger fish swim swiftly to the bigger food

4. Some fish don't care about the food.

   Some particular fish don't care about the very nasty food.

5. The owner taps on the side of the aquarium to get the fish's attention.

   The confused owner dramatically ~~frantically~~ taps on the glassy side of the aquarium to get the fish's attention.

B. Writing with Adjectives and Adverbs

On the lines below, write a description of the hallways in your school between classes. Who is walking there? How do the people look? How do they sound? As you walk through the hall, what can you smell or feel? In your description, use at least five adjectives and five adverbs. Underline the adjectives once and the adverbs twice.

Class changes at Roosevelt can only be described as a little on the chaotic side. Every student has a starting place, location and route to take. The halls are often clogged w/ bustling of Molasis like groups. The people look distracted yet focused on getting somewhere. The noise is

Prepositions

Teaching

A **preposition** shows the relationship between a noun or pronoun and some other word in the sentence. A preposition always introduces a phrase called a **prepositional phrase**. A prepositional phrase ends in a noun or a pronoun called the **object of the preposition**. Any modifiers of the object are also part of the prepositional phrase.

> Bridges connect the two sides <u>of</u> a traveler's <u>obstacle</u>. (The preposition is *of*, the object of the preposition is *obstacle*.)

A **compound preposition** is a preposition that consists of more than one word. The following are some compound prepositions: *according to, in addition to, prior to, in spite of, aside from, in place of*, and *by means of*. **Compound objects** are two or more objects of a single proposition.

> Bridges cross rivers and lakes <u>in addition to</u> <u>canyons</u> and <u>highways</u>.
> COMPOUND   COMPOUND OBJECT
> PREPOSITION

Finding Prepositions

Underline the preposition in each sentence. Remember that compound prepositions have two or more words. Double underline the object or objects of the preposition.

1. Logs thrown across rivers were probably the first bridges.
2. However, not every chasm can be bridged by a single log.
3. People who traveled eventually felt a need for more sophisticated bridges.
4. Historians tell of an early Babylonian bridge.
5. This first arch bridge was built around 2200 B.C. using bricks and stones.
6. During the Middle Ages, early engineers built moveable bridges.
7. Friendly visitors could enter the castle over these bridges, which would be raised when necessary.
8. Early engineers built most bridges of stone or wood.
9. After the 1700s, they used cast iron and wrought iron more extensively.
10. During the 1800s, engineers built the first suspension bridges.
11. A suspension bridge's main span stretches between two towers.
12. Sometimes suspension bridges sway in heavy winds.
13. They can be strengthened with girders or trusses.
14. The famous Golden Gate Bridge in San Francisco is a suspension bridge.
15. Every day thousands of drivers cross another suspension bridge, the Brooklyn Bridge.
16. New York's Brooklyn Bridge was designed by John Roebling.
17. In spite of many difficulties, he and his son and wife completed the project.
18. When it was finally completed, this bridge was the longest suspension bridge in the world.
19. Many other bridges now surpass it in length.
20. For example, the Mackinac Bridge is 18,615 feet long while the Brooklyn Bridge is only 5,989 feet long.

Review 5

Prepositions

More Practice

A. Identifying Prepositions

Underline once each preposition. Double underline the object of the preposition. A sentence may have more than one prepositional phrase.

1. Sarah works at a guitar factory near Kalamazoo, Michigan.
2. The ichthyologists were fascinated by the exotic fish in the aquarium.
3. Jane Austen received many rejections from publishers.
4. Water evaporates slowly when its temperature is below the boiling point.
5. I often get lox and bagels at the delicatessen near my house.
6. Cindy excels at field hockey in addition to tennis.
7. Prior to the Industrial Revolution, most products were made in people's homes.
8. I haven't met the family who bought the house across the street.
9. May I have fried rice in place of the white rice listed on the menu?
10. Sirius and Canopus are among the brightest stars in the universe.

B. Writing with Prepositional Phrases

Underline the prepositional phrase in each sentence. Then replace that phrase and write a new sentence on the line. Use the preposition provided in parentheses and a new object of the preposition.

EXAMPLE Have you ever driven over the Mackinac Bridge? (into)
Have you ever driven into New York City?

1. This bridge stands between Lake Michigan and Lake Huron. (over)

_____

2. Have you ever seen a suspension bridge like this one? (in)

_____

3. It was built in 1957. (with)

_____

4. The bridge has become famous on account of its tremendous length. (because of)

_____

5. The bridge was constructed over a three-year period. (for)

_____

6. It can withstand the strongest winds of winter. (in)

_____

Review 5

Prepositions

A. Writing with Prepositional Phrases

Add one or more prepositional phrases to each simple sentence. Write your new sentence on the line.

1. The driver approached the bridge.

_____

2. She paid a toll.

_____

3. Carefully, she drove and looked.

_____

4. The traffic was heavy.

_____

5. Other cars passed hers.

_____

6. She saw private boats and ocean-going ships.

_____

B. Writing with Prepositional Phrases

Use six of these prepositional phrases in an original story. Write your story on the lines below.

behind the secret door   after the storm   in addition to the guard dogs
below the stairs   in the firelight   within the gates
among the flowers   in spite of her fear   from the cellar

_____

_____

_____

_____

_____

_____

_____

_____

Review 6

Conjunctions and Interjections

Teaching

A **conjunction** is a word used to join words or groups of words.

Type of Conjunction	Function	Examples
coordinating	connects words or word groups that have equal importance in a sentence	and, but, or, for, so, yet, nor
correlative	pairs of conjunctions that connect words or groups of words	both . . . and, either . . . or, neither . . . nor, not only . . . but also, whether . . . or
subordinating	introduces a subordinate clause— a clause that cannot stand alone as complete	after, because, before, in order that, since, until, when, wherever, while

A **conjunctive adverb** is an adverb used as a coordinating conjunction to clarify the relationship between clauses of equal weight. Examples include *besides, finally, however, otherwise, still, then,* and *therefore.*

An **interjection** is a word or short phrase used to express emotion, such as *wow* and *my goodness.* It has no grammatical connection to other words in a sentence. Interjections are usually set off from the rest of the sentence by a comma or an exclamation point.

Identifying Conjunctions and Interjections

In the following sentences, underline the conjunctions once and conjunctive adverbs twice. Draw parentheses around interjections. Remember that there are two parts to a correlative conjunction.

1. Both meat and eggs are rich in protein.

2. The movie turned out to be much less exciting than we had expected. Oh, well.

3. William Canby insisted his grandmother Betsy Ross had made the first United States flag, but most historians do not support that claim.

4. Since I cannot find a dress I like, I will have to sew one myself.

5. Oh, no! Lucero sprained her ankle in practice; otherwise, she would have been a contender for first place in that race.

6. Forests are important not only for the products they supply, but also for their environmental value.

7. I went to bed early, yet I could not fall asleep.

8. Because we brought along our own bottles of water, we had something to drink.

9. I could not decide whether I wanted the strawberry ice cream or the watermelon sherbet.

10. Tyler wanted to learn how to administer emergency medical treatment; therefore, he took a first-aid class.

11. Sara waved her hand wildly; finally, she caught the attention of the speaker.

12. Neither this coffee nor the herbal tea has any caffeine.

13. The tickets had already been sold out when we arrived at the theater.

14. The forecaster predicted rain, so remember your umbrella.

15. Benjamin Franklin was not only an inventor and a printer, but also a diplomat and statesman. Incredible!

Review 6

Conjunctions and Interjections

More Practice

A. Identifying Conjunctions, Conjunctive Adverbs, and Interjections

In the following sentences, underline the conjunctions once and conjunctive adverbs twice. Draw parentheses around interjections.

1. Stir the paint properly, or the color will not be uniform.
2. Onomatopoeia is used not only in poetry but also in our daily speech.
3. Both the toad and the frog are amphibians.
4. The weekend is supposed to be cold; however, we still want to go camping.
5. Remember to clean your brushes thoroughly so that they last a long time.
6. Oops, I didn't realize I was standing on your foot.
7. A peacock has a beautiful fan of feathers, but the feathers are not its true tail.
8. Yipes! I just don't believe this could be happening!
9. Because the competition is 200 miles away, we must leave early.
10. As long as the water looked clear, we thought it safe to drink.

B. Using Conjunctions, Conjunctive Adverbs, and Interjections

Complete each of the following sentences with a conjunction, a conjunctive adverb, or an interjection.

EXAMPLE Several test questions were difficult, *but* I think I did well.

1. _____ ice skating _____ skiing appeals to me because I hate cold weather.

2. Butter the dish thoroughly; _____, the soufflé will stick to it.

3. The ballgame was postponed _____ a huge thunderstorm drenched the field.

4. The Siberian tiger is an endangered species; _____, steps are being taken to ensure its survival.

5. Whether Sheila wins the prize _____ is named runner-up depends on how well she performs today.

6. _____ the day was bright and spring like, most workers longed to be outdoors.

7. _____ cherry pie _____ apple pie would make a great dessert.

8. _____ it rains that day, we will have the art fair outside.

Review 6 Conjunctions and Interjections   *Application*

A. Proofreading
Proofread the following paragraph, adding appropriate conjunctions and conjunctive adverbs where they are needed.

_____ I stepped up to the plate, the score was 5 to 4. It was

the bottom of the ninth inning, there was a man on third base,

_____ two outs had already been made. I was under a lot of

pressure, _____ I did not like it. _____ I would get

a hit, _____ I would strike out. _____ we would win

this game _____ lose it was up to me. I wished someone else

could bat; _____, it was my turn. The pitcher looked me over for

a few moments; _____, he threw the ball. _____!

I hit a solid line drive to right field! I was _____ happy,

_____ I was _____ very proud. _____!

B. Writing a Conversation Using Conjunctions and Interjections
Imagine the conversation that Orville and Wilbur Wright might have had on the historic day when they flew their engine-powered airplane for the first time. On the lines below, write the conversation as you imagine it. Use at least two coordinating conjunctions, one correlative conjunction, two subordinating conjunctions, one conjunctive adverb, and one interjection. Below the conversation, list the conjunctions, conjunctive adverb, and interjections you used under the appropriate headings.

_____

_____

_____

_____

_____

_____

Coordinating Conjunctions   **Correlative Conjunctions**

_____   _____

_____   **Conjunctive Adverbs**

Subordinating Conjunctions   _____

_____   **Interjections**

_____   _____

                                                 _____

Subjects and Predicates

Teaching

A **sentence** is a group of words that expresses a complete thought. A complete sentence has a subject and a predicate. The most basic elements of a sentence are the simple subject and the simple predicate. The **simple subject** tells who or what performs the action in a sentence. The **simple predicate,** or **verb,** tells what the subject did or what happened to the subject.

Ichabod Crane <u>taught</u> in the Sleepy Hollow schoolhouse.
SIMPLE   SIMPLE
SUBJECT   PREDICATE

The **complete subject** includes the simple subject and all the words that modify it. The **complete predicate** includes all the words that tell what the subject did or what happened to the subject.

<u>The people of Sleepy Hollow</u> <u>respected their learned schoolmaster.</u>
COMPLETE SUBJECT   COMPLETE PREDICATE

A **sentence fragment** is a group of words that is only part of a sentence. It may lack a subject, a predicate, or both.

A. Identifying Subjects and Predicates

If the simple subject is boldfaced, write **SS** on the line. If the simple predicate is boldfaced, write **SP.** Write **CS** if the boldfaced words are the complete subject and **CP** if they are the complete predicate.

1. Ichabod Crane **had come to Sleepy Hollow from Connecticut.** _____

2. The **schoolmaster** lived with a different family every week. _____

3. He **enjoyed** the hospitality and good cooking of the neighborhood housewives. _____

4. **This nervous man** was quite superstitious and fearful of shapes in the shadows. _____

5. Crane **fell** in love with the beautiful Katrina Van Tassel, the daughter of a wealthy Dutch farmer. _____

6. Crane's **rival** for the affections of Katrina was local hero Brom Van Brunt. _____

7. One dark night in the forest, **Ichabod Crane** was terrorized by a figure on horseback, the ghost of a headless horseman. _____

8. The frightened schoolmaster **disappeared that night after a desperate chase through the woods.** _____

B. Identifying Complete Sentences

Read each of the following groups of words. If the words form a complete sentence, write **CS** on the line. If the words form a sentence fragment, write **F,** and tell whether the fragment is missing a subject **(MS)** or a predicate **(MP)** or both **(MSP).**

1. Washington Irving, one of the first American writers. _____

2. Told the story of Ichabod Crane in "The Legend of Sleepy Hollow." _____

3. This short story has become an American classic. _____

4. In the quiet New York village of Sleepy Hollow with distinctly American characters. _____

Subjects and Predicates

More Practice

A. Identifying Subjects and Predicates

Draw a vertical line between the complete subject and the complete predicate. Then underline the simple subject once and the simple predicate twice.

EXAMPLE <u>People</u> of Pawley Island | <u><u>tell</u></u> a story of a helpful apparition.

1. Pawley Island, South Carolina, is a beachcomber's paradise.
2. Its beautiful beaches attract ocean enthusiasts throughout the year.
3. The island often lies on the pathways of severe storms and hurricanes.
4. The Gray Man of Pawley Island appears before every major storm.
5. The sight of this helpful ghost warns residents of approaching bad weather.
6. Residents of the island reported sightings of the Gray Man before Hurricane Hazel in 1954.
7. The elusive Gray Man is dressed all in gray, with a long jacket and a strange hat.
8. The most amazing characteristic of the apparition is that he has no face.
9. According to local legend, the man may be the ghost of a veteran of the American Revolution.
10. This mysterious figure appeared before storms in 1822, 1893, 1916, and 1954.

B. Using Complete Subjects and Predicates

On the line to the right of each item, write how each of the following groups of words could be used: **CS** for a complete subject or **CP** for a complete predicate. Then use each group of words to write a complete sentence, adding a complete subject or a complete predicate as necessary.

EXAMPLE hiked to the bottom of the canyon and back   *CP*

The enthusiastic tourists hiked to the bottom of the canyon and back.

1. animals of the desert   _____

_____

2. photographed natural wonders   _____

_____

3. the strange case of the missing parakeet   _____

_____

4. forgot the words to the national anthem before the ball game _____

_____

5. nachos with salsa   _____

_____

6. made cookies for the school bake sale   _____

_____

CHAPTER 1

Subjects and Predicates

Application

Lesson 1

A. Writing Subjects and Predicates

Write sentences on the lines below by adding both a subject and a predicate to each fragment. Do not use the fragment as the subject of the sentence.

EXAMPLE the light of the harvest moon *Farmers work by the light of the harvest moon.*

1. after the homecoming dance

_____

_____

2. the steps to a new dance

_____

_____

3. in a bottle on the shelf in the basement

_____

_____

4. a thoroughbred race horse

_____

_____

5. beyond the furthest planet of the solar system

_____

_____

B. Revising

Read this paragraph carefully. It contains several sentence fragments. When you find a sentence fragment, insert this proofreading symbol ⌄ and write the words necessary to complete the sentence above the symbol.

EXAMPLE In 1843 the writer Charles Dickens ⌄*wrote* the popular tale, *A Christmas Carol*.

    A Christmas Carol a story about a bitter, selfish, mean old man named

Ebenezer Scrooge. The ghost of his former partner, Jacob Marley, visits him at

night. Marley Scrooge that three spirits will visit him that night. First, a ghost

who shows Scrooge how he had been as a young boy. Second, a ghost who

shows Scrooge himself in the present arrives. This ghost shows Scrooge the

home of his employee, Bob Cratchit. Indeed, does not pay Cratchit well

enough to support his large family. Last, a ghost shows Scrooge his future. It

is gloomy and depressing. The ghosts have taught Scrooge how his behavior

has hurt those around him.

Lesson 2

Compound Sentence Parts

Teaching

A **compound subject** is made up of two or more subjects that share a verb. The subjects are joined by a conjunction, or connecting word, such as *and, or,* or *but*.

<u>Juniors</u> and <u>seniors</u> are working on a project.

A **compound verb** is made up of two or more verbs or verb phrases that are joined by a conjunction and share the same subject. They may also share the same direct objects.

They <u>meet</u> and <u>plan</u>.

A **compound predicate** includes a compound verb and all the words that go with each verb.

The classes <u>chose a leader</u> and <u>outlined their goals</u>.

Identifying Subjects and Verbs

In each sentence, underline the simple subject(s) once and the verb(s) twice. Write **CS** if the sentence has a compound subject or **CV** if it has a compound verb. The sentences with compound predicates have already been identified.

EXAMPLE <u>Faculty</u> and <u>students</u> <u>are</u> excited about a time capsule _____CS_____

1. The students and teachers at Valley High School recently buried a time capsule. _____

2. The faculty organized and planned a time capsule contest for the students. _____

3. Participants picked an object and then explained the reasons for their choice. ____CP____

4. Newspapers and magazines were chosen most frequently. _____

5. The history teacher liked the choice but demanded the right of final approval of the reading material. ____CP____

6. Both CDs and video games were chosen by quite a few of the students as well. _____

7. A few of the students selected and defended different choices. _____

8. One student liked a particular cologne and wanted a bottle of it in the capsule for a fragrant package. ____CP____

9. The faculty read the suggestions and chose some unusual objects themselves. ____CP____

10. Running shoes and a gym membership card were also included in the capsule. _____

11. Fat-free potato chips were chosen but were eaten by some faculty members prior to the burial of the capsule. _____

12. A pair of khaki pants and an advertisement for an Internet service provider were selected last. _____

CHAPTER 1

Lesson 2 # Compound Sentence Parts   *More Practice*

A. Identifying Compound Sentence Parts

All of these sentences have either a compound subject, a compound verb, or a compound predicate. In every sentence, underline simple subject(s) once and the verb(s) twice.

> **EXAMPLE** Tiny <u>wristwatches</u> and grandfather <u>clocks</u> <u>have</u> one thing in common.

1. Clocks keep and show the time.
2. Timepieces may swing a pendulum or may record the vibrations of atoms.
3. Atomic clocks lose or gain no more than a second every 250,000 years.
4. Churches and public buildings often display the time to passersby.
5. The Chinese probably invented the first mechanical clock but did not develop their invention completely.

B. Using Compound Subjects, Compound Verbs, and Compound Predicates

Combine the sentence pairs to form a new sentence with the sentence part indicated in parentheses. Use the conjunction *(either . . . or; neither . . . nor; and, or, nor,* or *but)* that makes the most sense.

> **EXAMPLE** The cheese and tomato pizza at the new restaurant is very tasty. The eggplant lasagna is also very tasty. (compound subject)
> *The cheese and tomato pizza and the eggplant lasagna at the new restaurant are very tasty.*

1. Gabriel did not walk the two puppies last night. He also did not bathe them last night. (compound verb)

   _____

2. The assistant typed the director's speech for the fundraising dinner. Then she printed it. (compound verb)

   _____

3. Joshua applied to five colleges in his senior year of high school. He did not get accepted into his first choice, though. (compound predicate)

   _____

4. The girls' soccer team did not lose a game last year. The boys' soccer team had the same record last year too. (compound subject)

   _____

5. Jerry enjoys helping people and wants to become a pediatrician after his graduation from college. Interestingly, his twin sister feels the same about her future. (compound subject and compound predicate)

   _____

CHAPTER 1

Compound Sentence Parts

Application

A. Sentence Combining with Compound Subjects, Compound Verbs, and Compound Predicates

Combine each pair of sentences by writing a compound subject, a compound verb, or a compound predicate. Be sure that the subject and the verb agree in number.

1. Science fiction authors imagine events in the future. Then, they write about these events.

_____

2. Boston is located in the Eastern Standard Time Zone. Miami is also in that time zone.

_____

3. In *The Time Machine* by H.G. Wells, the main character travels to the near future of World War I and World War II. The main character also visits a time 800,000 years into the future.

_____

4. Sailors use Greenwich Mean Time (GMT). Astronomers use it as well.

_____

5. Standard time, which was introduced in 1883, cleared up complications in railroad schedules. It required all clocks in one time zone to be set to the same time.

_____

B. More Sentence Combining

Revise the following paragraph, using compound subjects, compound verbs, and compound predicates to combine sentences with similar ideas. Write the new paragraph on the lines below. Use an additional piece of paper if needed.

> Foreign Service Officers are people who work for the State Department. Foreign Service Officers solve problems involving U.S. relations with other countries. They may work in Washington, D.C. They may also be sent abroad to any country. Foreign Service Officers study foreign trends. They develop new policies for the U.S. government. The President relies on the State Department and the Secretary of State for information and advice on foreign policy. Members of the House of Representatives and the Senate turn to the State Department for information and advice too. Formulating and directing foreign policy has become more complicated during the past century. It will demand more informed and better-trained officers.

_____

_____

_____

_____

_____

Lesson 3

Kinds of Sentences   *Teaching*

There are four types of sentences, each with a specific function. In most sentences, the subject comes before the verb. A **declarative sentence** expresses a statement of fact, wish, intent, or feeling. An **interrogative sentence** asks a question. An **imperative sentence** gives a command, request, or direction. An **exclamatory sentence** expresses strong feeling.

declarative	The Great Depression was a worldwide phenomenon.
interrogative	How did the Depression affect the United States?
imperative	Explain the reasons for the Depression.
exclamatory	How terrible it was for those who lost their jobs!

Identifying Kinds of Sentences

Insert appropriate end punctuation after each sentence below. On the line to the right of each sentence, identify the sentence as **DEC** for declarative, **INT** for interrogative, **IMP** for imperative, or **EXC** for exclamatory.

1. The 1920s had been a time of prosperity and high hopes _____

2. Millions of Americans invested heavily in the stock market _____

3. Was the stock market crash of 1929 totally unexpected, or could it have been predicted ahead of time _____

4. How devastated the small and large investors must have been when their stocks plummeted in value _____

5. Imagine going to the bank and being told that you could not withdraw your money _____

6. Savers were faced with this upsetting development after the banks failed during the late 1920s and early 1930s _____

7. How could people buy anything without being able to withdraw their money from the bank _____

8. People not only stopped buying extras, but they also were not able to pay their house mortgages or food bills _____

9. Picture the homeless trying to live in the streets of big cities _____

10. Think about the poor farmers who had experienced money troubles for years, even before the stock market crash _____

11. What more could go wrong for these people _____

12. A prolonged dry spell turned the central section of the United States into a Dust Bowl _____

13. The rich topsoil blew away, leaving farmers with no possibility of income for years _____

Lesson 3 **Kinds of Sentences**   *More Practice*

A. Writing Different Kinds of Sentences

Label each sentence below as **DEC** for declarative, **INT** for interrogative, **IMP** for imperative, or **EXC** for exclamatory. Then write a sentence of your own of the same kind.

> **EXAMPLE** Factories and businesses shut their doors. *DEC*
> *No one had the money to buy new products.*

1. The Great Depression caused much suffering.

_____

2. How strange it must have been to be suddenly poor!

_____

3. Were your grandparents or great-grandparents affected by the Depression?

_____

4. Put yourself in the position of those who lived through the Depression.

_____

5. Experiences during the Depression changed how some people treated money.

_____

B. Writing Different Kinds of Sentences

On the line to the right, identify each sentence as **DEC** for declarative, **INT** for interrogative, **IMP** for imperative, or **EXC** for exclamatory. Then rewrite the sentences according to the instructions in parentheses. You may have to add or delete words and change word order.

> **EXAMPLE** Will you show me where to sign this form? *INT*
> (Change to an imperative sentence.)
> *Show me where to sign this form.*

1. The plane will depart at 8:22 a.m. (Change to an interrogative sentence.)   _____

_____

2. We will arrive at the airport one hour before take-off.   _____
(Change to an imperative sentence.)

_____

3. The plane is crowded this morning.   (Change to an exclamatory sentence.)   _____

_____

4. How fluffy the clouds look! (Change to an declarative sentence.)   _____

_____

Kinds of Sentences

Application

A. Writing Different Kinds of Sentences in a Diary Entry

Imagine that you had been alive during the Depression and suddenly found yourself without an income. Write a diary entry from the day when you lost your job. Use at least one of each of the following types of sentences: declarative, interrogative, imperative, and exclamatory. Use the correct punctuation at the end of each sentence.

_____

_____

_____

_____

_____

_____

_____

_____

B. Writing Different Kinds of Sentences in a Dialogue

Write a dialogue that two students might have after a difficult test. Use at least one of each kind of sentence: declarative, interrogative, imperative, and exclamatory. Enclose each speaker's words in quotation marks. Use the correct punctuation at the end of each sentence, inside the quotation marks.

_____

_____

_____

_____

_____

_____

_____

_____

_____

CHAPTER 1

Lesson 4 **Subjects in Unusual Positions** *Teaching*

Usually, the subject in a sentence comes before the verb. However, in some sentences, the order is reversed.

In an **inverted sentence,** the verb or part of the verb phrase is stated before the subject. An inverted sentence can be used for variety or emphasis.

> Under the ground lie the tulip bulbs.
>   VERB   SUBJECT

When a sentence begins with **here** or **there,** the subject usually follows the verb.

> There are six flowering trees in my garden.

In most **questions,** the subject appears between the words that make up the verb phrase.

> Were the bulbs planted in the spring? (The subject interrupts the verb phrase *were planted.*)

In **imperative sentences and commands,** the subject is usually understood to be *you.*

> (You) Plant tulip bulbs about two inches deep.

Finding Subjects and Verbs in Sentences

In the following sentences, underline the simple subject once and the verb or verb phrase twice. If the subject is understood, write *You* in parentheses on the line.

1. There are 12 tea roses along the fence in the garden. _____

2. Dig the hole for the bush one foot deep and two feet wide. _____

3. Will Shasta daisies grow in the shade? _____

4. Over the rocks cascaded the purple phlox. _____

5. Here are the necessary gardening tools for the job. _____

6. Use a trellis for the climbing roses. _____

7. Have you planned the herb garden yet? _____

8. Among the pine trees gleamed the white lilies. _____

9. Transplant the hostas to the back of the garden. _____

10. Here was last year's vegetable garden. _____

11. Through the blanket of snow peeked yellow and purple crocuses. _____

12. Can this hydrangea survive another year? _____

13. Spread the pine bark mulch over the entire area. _____

14. Around the pond grew tall sedges. _____

CHAPTER 1

Lesson 4

Subjects in Unusual Positions

More Practice

A. Writing Sentences

In the following sentences, underline the simple subject once and the verb twice. Then rewrite each sentence so that the subject comes before the verb.

EXAMPLE Here are the missing puzzle <u>pieces.</u>
The missing puzzle pieces are here.

1. Hanging from the vines all around us were juicy grapes.

   _____

2. There is a strange odor coming from the kitchen.

   _____

3. Will the school orchestra travel to Europe this spring?

   _____

4. Here are the statistics you asked for earlier today.

   _____

5. From a crack in the sidewalk grew a delicate flower.

   _____

B. Writing Sentences

Rewrite these sentences, following the directions in parentheses. Underline the simple subject of your sentence once and the verb twice. If the subject is an understood *you*, write *You* in parentheses after your sentence.

EXAMPLE The roses are here. (Begin with *Here.*)
Here are the roses.

1. You must water impatiens almost every day to insure maximum growth. (Change this to an imperative sentence.)

   _____

2. I work in my garden for about an hour each day. (Change the sentence to a question.)

   _____

3. Weeds are growing between the rows of marigolds. (Begin with *There.*)

   _____

4. Behind the shed are the extra clay pots. (Begin with the words *The extra.* Use a traditional word order.)

   _____

5. Will you move to a warm climate for year-round enjoyment of your flower garden? (Change this to an imperative sentence.)

   _____

CHAPTER 1

Subjects in Unusual Positions

Lesson 4

Application

A. Revising Using a Variety of Sentence Types

The writer of this paragraph decided to use only declarative sentences with the traditional word order of subject before verb. Rewrite the paragraph, this time using a variety of kinds of sentences, including those arranged in the traditional order of subject before verb and at least two in which the verb comes before the subject. Use an additional piece of paper if necessary.

> Gardening is a favorite pastime of millions of Americans. They spend countless amounts of time and money to beautify their surroundings. Some people plant only low-maintenance perennial gardens. (Perennials are plants that grow year after year.) Others enjoy the wide variety of annual plants. (Annuals live for one season only.) Trees and shrubs are more permanent additions to the landscape. These long-lasting plants must be chosen carefully. They will thrive if planted in the proper location and given the right care.

_____

_____

_____

_____

_____

_____

B. Revising Using a Variety of Sentence Orders

The writer of this paragraph decided to use both traditional word order of subject before verb and a less traditional inverted sentence order. Rewrite the paragraph, this time using a variety of sentence orders to make it more understandable and pleasing to the reader. Use an additional piece of paper if necessary.

> Have you ever seen a gardening show on TV? Always perfect are the gardens, filled with masses of gorgeous flowers. Not so is my garden. Flowers have I, and also plenty of hungry bugs and nasty fungi. Favorite snacks of the borers are my iris corms. There are gourmet rabbits who nibble on the tulips. Adept at moving the daffodil bulbs are the squirrels. Tunneling under them, chipmunks uproot the annuals. My garden definitely is not a showplace—it is a wildlife deli.

_____

_____

_____

_____

_____

CHAPTER 1

Lesson 5

Subject Complements

Teaching

Complements are words or groups of words that complete the meaning of verbs.

Subject complements are words that follow linking verbs and describe or rename the subjects. Subject complements often come after a form of the verb *be*.

Predicate adjectives are adjectives that follow linking verbs and describe subjects.

> This folktale <u>is</u> quite <u>old</u>. (*Old* describes *folktales*. The linking verb is *is*.)

Predicate nominatives are nouns or pronouns that follow linking verbs and rename, identify, or define subjects.

> Myths <u>are</u> <u>stories</u> that explain natural phenomena. (*Stories* describes *myths*.)

Identifying Linking Verbs and Subject Complements

Underline the linking verb in each sentence. On the line, identify the boldfaced complement as a predicate nominative **(PN)** or a predicate adjective **(PA)**.

1. Folklore is the **set** of beliefs and customs passed down from one generation to the next. _____

2. Most children are **happy** when their parents tuck them into bed with a folktale. _____

3. Fables are an ever-popular **form** of folklore. _____

4. The main characters in many fables may be **animals** who can talk. _____

5. Some of these characters, such as the fox, are **famous** for their cleverness and slyness. _____

6. The settings for folktales have traditionally been **indefinite**, not set in any particular place or time. _____

7. In African folktales, a sly spider named Anansi is often the **subject** of the story. _____

8. Some tales of monsters and giants can be **scary** to small children. _____

9. Many Asian folktales seem exceedingly **long**, taking all day to relate. _____

10. Children's games, such as leapfrog and marbles, are a **type** of folklore passed on by imitation. _____

11. Proverbs are wise **sayings** handed down from generation to generation. _____

12. Proverbs may be quite **short**; just a few meaningful words convey the message. _____

13. Such sayings can be quite **effective** in teaching a lesson. _____

14. A folk story may be **universal**, that is, found in some version throughout the world. _____

15. Variations in a story or song are an important **sign** that it is authentic folklore.

Subject Complements

Lesson 5

More Practice

A. Identifying Subject Complements

In each of the following sentences, underline the linking verb once and the subject complement twice. Then, in the blank, write **PN** if the subject complement is a **predicate nominative** or **PA** if it is a **predicate adjective**.

1. A flag can be a symbol of a nation's people, territory, and heritage. _____

2. Other banners are signs of various organizations, such as the UN or the Boy Scouts. _____

3. Flags of various colors and designs can be message senders, as well. _____

4. The use of banners is quite ancient, dating to the Egyptians. _____

5. Flags of the Roman Army were easy for the soldiers and generals to see in battle. _____

6. The colors and symbols of a flag usually are important to that nation's history. _____

7. Stars on a banner often are a mark of unity. _____

8. Regional flags were abundant in the colonies before the Revolutionary War. _____

9. Our state flags are part of our country's history. _____

10. Ohio's flag is triangular, the only state flag so shaped. _____

B. Using Subject Complements

Complete each sentence below in two ways. First complete it with a predicate nominative. Then complete it with a predicate adjective.

> **EXAMPLE** The legend is *an American classic.*
> The legend is *unbelievable.*

1. The logging giant Paul Bunyan was _____.

   The logging giant Paul Bunyan was _____.

2. Storytellers are often _____.

   Storytellers are often _____.

3. The main character in a legend may be _____.

   The main character in a legend may be _____.

4. People who research fables and legends are _____.

   People who research fables and legends are _____.

5. A modern, urban legend might be _____.

   A modern, urban legend might be _____.

CHAPTER 1

Subject Complements   *Application*

A. Writing with Subject Complements

Using words from the columns below, write six sentences with subject complements.
You may use each word only once, and you must use all the words. You may change
the form of a verb. Add other words to make your sentences interesting.

Nouns	Verbs	Adjectives
castle	is	strong
dragons	appears	fiery
princess	was	grateful
kingdom	have been	handsome
prince	seems	lovely
armor	were	shiny

1. _____

2. _____

3. _____

4. _____

5. _____

6. _____

B. Writing Subject Complements

Complete each sentence in the following passage with either a predicate
nominative or a predicate adjective. Following your sentence, write **PN** if you have
used a predicate nominative or **PA** if you have completed the sentence with a
predicate adjective.

(1) Relating a folktale can be _____. **(2)** Your intonation and

gestures are _____. **(3)** Keeping the attention of the audience is

_____. **(4)** Whispering and rustling may be _____.

(5) Memorizing the story may be _____. **(6)** A sure-fire way to

end the tale is _____.

1. _____

2. _____

3. _____

4. _____

5. _____

6. _____

CHAPTER 1

Lesson 6 # Objects of Verbs *Teaching*

Like subject complements, **object complements** are words or groups of words that complete the meaning of verbs.

A **direct object** is a noun or pronoun that receives the action of an action verb. It may be one word or may consist of a phrase or a clause.

> Searchers <u>can</u> find almost <u>anything</u> on the Internet.

> You <u>can</u> find <u>whatever you are looking for</u> within a few minutes.

An **indirect object** is a word or a group of words that tells *to whom* or *for whom* the action of the verb is being performed. Verbs that often take indirect objects include *bring, give, hand, lend, make, offer, send, show, teach, tell,* and *write.*

> This site offers <u>readers</u> a list of related Web sites.

An **objective complement** is a noun or adjective that follows the direct object and identifies or describes it. Only a few verbs and their synonyms can be followed by objective complements; these verbs include *appoint, call, choose, consider, elect, find, keep, make, name, render,* and *think.*

> Many consumers find Internet sites <u>indispensable</u>.

Identifying Objects of Verbs

On the line, identify the boldfaced word as a direct object **(DO),** an indirect object **(IO),** or an objective complement **(OC).**

1. Highly motivated consumers consider Internet shopping **incomparable.** _____

2. Rodney purchased the lowest priced airline **tickets** through the Internet. _____

3. Web page links gave **him** other useful sources of information. _____

4. A virus contracted from the Internet attacked the **data** stored in Claire's computer. _____

5. Observation of most Internet users would find them **guilty** of wasting quite a bit of time. _____

6. The Internet brings the **user** a virtual shopping mall. _____

7. Jackie located the **article** that she needed by using the Web browser. _____

8. Surfing the net became such an obsession with Paul that his mother appointed one of his siblings **watchdog** over his computer use. _____

9. Rather than writing individual letters, Ann sent her **friends** an e-mail message. _____

10. With her notebook computer Ms. Worthington could send her **clients** the necessary information by e-mail even when traveling. _____

11. An Internet service provides **access** to the Internet for a fee. _____

Objects of Verbs

More Practice

A. Identifying Objects of Verbs

In each of the following sentences, underline any objects of the verb. Then identify them further by writing in the space above **DO** for direct object, **IO** for indirect object, or **OC** for objective complement. Some sentences have more than one object of the verb.

1. Many people consider Winslow Homer one of the world's greatest artists.
2. Homer's magazine illustrations of the Civil War battles brought him fame.
3. His watercolors of sea scenes, however, made him popular.
4. His paintings showed his audience the inherent dangers of seafaring.
5. *The Life Line* depicts people struggling to survive a shipwreck.
6. Homer gave us other masterful seascapes, such as *Breaking Storm*.
7. Many observers find his seascapes rich in technique and emotional depth.

B. Using Indirect Objects

Underline the direct object in each sentence below. Then rewrite each sentence, adding an indirect object. Use a different indirect object for every sentence.

1. On my friend's birthday, I sent a digital greeting over the Internet.

_____

2. Show how to download a CD from the net.

_____

3. The Internet offers a convenient way to communicate with others.

_____

4. The computer salesperson made an offer that was quite attractive.

_____

5. Online malls can bring catalogs of available products.

_____

6. Send an e-mail message from your hotel.

_____

CHAPTER 1

Lesson 6 **Objects of Verbs**   *Application*

A. Using Complements in Sentences

Choose one word from each list below to complete each sentence. Use each item
only once. Each sentence should have both an indirect object and a direct object. If
you wish, you can add words to make the sentences more interesting.

Use as indirect object	Use as direct object
her penpal	a tip
his teacher	the newspaper
his neighbor	a story
her friend	a letter
his master	the homework assignment
the paper carrier	a refund
the preschoolers	an afghan
the passenger	a ladder

1. A cab driver offered _____.

2. The elderly gentleman lent _____.

3. Grandmother made _____.

4. He handed _____.

5. The librarian read _____.

6. Linda wrote _____.

7. Mr. Cummings gave _____.

8. The sheepdog brought _____.

B. Writing Sentences with Objects of Verbs

Complete each sentence with an objective complement—either a noun or an
adjective. You may also add additional words to make the sentence clearer and
more interesting.

> **EXAMPLE** Online I have given myself *a new name*.

1. I consider talking to my friends online _____.

2. Sheila calls her parakeet _____.

3. Many people find the Internet _____.

4. The committee elected Ryan _____.

5. The all-day hike rendered the tourists _____.

6. The principal appointed Gina _____.

Lesson 7 # Sentence Diagramming

Complete each diagram with the sentence provided.

A. Subjects and Verbs

Simple Subject and Verb
Travelers sightsee.

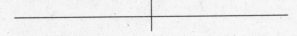

Compound Subject
Travelers and merchants converse.

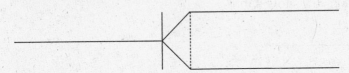

Compound Verb
Travelers observe and compare.

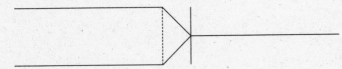

B. Adjectives and Adverbs
The eager visitors talked excitedly.

C. Subject Complements: Predicate Nominatives and Predicate Adjectives

Predicate Nominative That ancient, oval structure is the famous Coliseum.

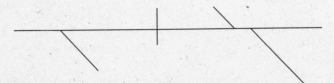

Predicate Adjective The Pantheon looks remarkably new.

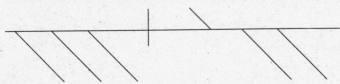

Sentence Diagramming

D. Direct and Indirect Objects, and Objective Complements

Direct Object My companions have been carrying cameras everywhere.

Compound Predicate I loved the scenery and shot still pictures and video.

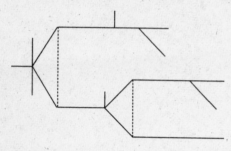

Indirect Object These famous buildings give visitors a thrill.

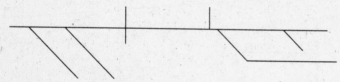

Objective Complement
The lovely Italian village held me spell-bound.

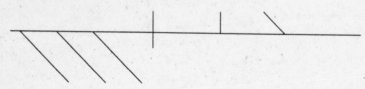

I considered our visit a memorable experience.

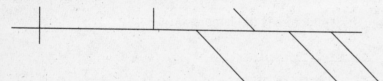

Lesson 7

Sentence Diagramming

Application

On a separate piece of paper, diagram each of the following sentences.

A. Diagramming Subjects, Verbs, Modifiers, and Subject Complements

1. Some tour itineraries are too full.
2. Classical monuments and medieval castles are popular destinations.
3. The students and their guides toured tirelessly.
4. The Roman traffic sounded deafeningly loud.

B. Diagramming Objects and Objective Complements

1. No one tour can show you every worthwhile scene.
2. Most travelers come back and enjoy more sights.
3. You and your group must pace yourselves.
4. The gorgeous sunset made the evening perfect.

C. Mixed Practice

1. The friendly shopkeepers speak many languages.
2. Have you seen the Trevi Fountain?
3. One legend calls this old prison haunted.
4. Local people consider that story absurd.
5. This ancient statue must have been beautiful once.
6. Archaeologists still uncover valuable relics and share their discoveries.
7. Movies and television programs can never completely capture the travel experience.
8. A helpful travel agent is planning our next trip and will send us brochures and current prices soon.

Lesson 1

Prepositional Phrases

Teaching

A **prepositional phrase** consists of a preposition, its object, and any modifiers of the object.

Cuckoos lay eggs <u>in sparrows' nests</u>. (The preposition is *in*.)

An **adjective phrase** is a prepositional phrase that acts as an adjective to modify a noun or a pronoun.

The bird <u>in that photo</u> is a cardinal. (The phrase modifies *bird*, telling which one.)

An **adverb phrase** is a prepositional phrase that modifies a verb, an adjective, or an adverb. It usually tells *when, where, how, why,* or *to what extent.*

The hummingbird moves <u>with speed</u>. (The phrase modifies *moves*, telling how.)

To avoid confusion, place a prepositional phrase as close as possible to the word or words it modifies.

A. Identifying Prepositional Phrases

Underline every prepositional phrase in each of these sentences.

EXAMPLE White storks nest <u>on rooftops</u> <u>in Holland and Poland</u>.

1. A penguin has air sacs beneath its skin that help it stay above water.
2. A folk tale from China tells of a nightingale that was a favorite of the emperor.
3. You can feed birds in winter and watch them in your backyard.
4. A pet bird that is angry with you will turn its back on you.
5. The eagle, a symbol of America, flies high above the earth.
6. A robin is known by its red and black colors and is found throughout the Midwest.
7. This survey locates all tern and skimmer colonies in Florida and determines the number of breeding places.
8. The bird was chased into our house by the cat and finally flew out the window.
9. The barred owl is common in southern swamps and widespread in northern woods.
10. Birds that live in those treetops are not afraid of people.

B. Identifying Words Modified by Prepositional Phrases

Underline once the prepositional phrase in each of the following sentences. Underline twice the word or words it modifies.

1. In his lifetime Jack London held many jobs.
2. Maine is the only state in the United States that adjoins only one other state.
3. Paloverde, a flowering shrub, grows along desert canyon edges.
4. Both express mail and priority parcel post are shipped by air.
5. The deepest spot in the Pacific Ocean is the Mariana Trench.
6. Those blue flowers under that beech tree are called grape hyacinth.
7. The reverse side of the nickel depicts Monticello.
8. The fruit peddler's cart rattled along the cobblestone street.

Lesson 1

Prepositional Phrases

More Practice

A. Identifying Prepositional Phrases

In each sentence, underline the word modified by the boldfaced prepositional phrase. On the blank, write **ADJ** or **ADV** to identify what kind of prepositional phrase it is.

1. To obtain photographs of birds **in natural settings,** focus on a branch or other favorite perch. _____

2. A bird's song in the morning alerts males **of the same species** that there is no room for them in that bird's territory. _____

3. Without regard to artistic value, making field sketches is valuable in helping people learn **about birds.** _____

4. The species of birds in each photograph is identified **in the caption.** _____

5. Almost anyone **with experience** in photographing birds can help our group. _____

6. Some people look for robins **in winter or early spring.** _____

7. An owner **with great patience** can train a parrot to speak with adequate clarity. _____

8. An eagle skimmed **across the lake,** grasping a wiggling trout in its talons. _____

9. The strong beak **of the red-headed woodpecker** easily drills through the bark of any tree. _____

10. **With nonchalant assurance** the blue jay dodged among the brambles and landed on the branch. _____

B. Identifying Misplaced Prepositional Phrases

Underline every prepositional phrase in each sentence once. If a phrase is misplaced, underline it twice.

EXAMPLE All of the drawers were full of old photos of the cabinet.

1. The cerebellum is located below the back part of the cerebrum.
2. In the mineral, the color in most precious gems results from impurities.
3. Many peaks rise over 10,000 feet of the Rocky Mountains.
4. Kampuchea was once called Cambodia, in Southeast Asia.
5. In the closet there are boxes of used toys for the toy collection.
6. A car passed me as I crossed the street with its lights flashing.
7. The scarecrow kept birds away from the garden in my father's clothes.
8. To reach the cafeteria, go down this hallway, up the steps to the right, and across the courtyard.
9. The costumes we needed for the play were stored in large boxes under the stage.
10. A petri dish between the lab tables slipped out of my hands and became wedged.

CHAPTER 2

Lesson 1 Prepositional Phrases

Application

A. Revising Sentences with Misplaced Prepositional Phrases

Rewrite each sentence, changing the position of one or more prepositional phrases so that the sentence is no longer confusing.

> **EXAMPLE** The sound of the woodpecker woke the baby in the oak tree.
> *The sound of the woodpecker in the oak tree woke the baby.*

1. There is a book about the nesting habits of hummingbirds on the top shelf.

_____

2. Arthur spoke to May about his rare bird after it arrived from New York on the phone.

_____

3. Under the reeds I observed a mallard and her ducklings in a nest.

_____

4. The soaring hawk spotted the tiny field mouse with its keen eyesight.

_____

5. Peacocks proudly strutted with iridescent feathers through the gardens.

_____

B. Using Prepositional Phrases as Modifiers

Rewrite each of the following sentences, replacing each boldfaced word or phrase with a prepositional phrase that clarifies the meaning of the sentence. You may need to place the prepositional phrase in a position different from the position of the boldfaced word.

1. The train leaving **then** goes **there**.

_____

2. **That** package should be delivered to the house **like that**.

_____

3. I always order my salad **that way**.

_____

4. All the dancers **like that** are supposed to be sunflowers **then**.

_____

5. Kathy read **that** book **then**.

_____

Lesson 2 # Appositive Phrases   *Teaching*

An **appositive** is a noun or pronoun that identifies or renames another noun or pronoun. An **appositive phrase** consists of an appositive plus its modifiers.

> On vacation, I met Janet, <u>a volunteer at Everglades National Park</u>. (The appositive is *volunteer*; the whole appositive phrase is underlined.)

An **essential,** or **restrictive appositive,** is needed to make the meaning of a sentence clear. Essential appositives are not set off by commas.

> The pamphlet <u>"Saving the Everglades"</u> is available at the information desk. ("Saving the Everglades" identifies which pamphlet.)

A **nonessential,** or **nonrestrictive appositive,** adds extra information to a sentence whose meaning is already clear. Nonessential appositives are set off by commas.

> The pamphlet describes Everglades National Park, <u>a national treasure</u>.

A. Identifying Appositives and Appositive Phrases

Underline the appositive or appositive phrase in each of the following sentences.

1. The Everglades, a shallow river rather than a marsh, is in Florida.
2. Its vast acreage, a stretch of grass and water, is home to a variety of animal life.
3. Visitors regularly spot roseate spoonbills, exotic water birds.
4. The flamingo, another bird abundant there, can also be seen wading in the water.
5. Everglades National Park, a protected wildlife habitat, was established in 1947.
6. The area has been threatened by a new difficulty, the growing population of Florida.
7. Some cities draw their water from aquifers, natural underground reservoirs.

B. Identifying Essential and Nonessential Appositives

Underline the appositive or appositive phrase in each sentence below. On the line, identify each phrase as **E** if it is essential or **NE** if it is nonessential. Add necessary commas.

1. The Babylonians the most famous lawmakers of ancient times devised
   edicts regarding water usage.   _____

2. None of the cargo of that ship valuables from the 1600s has been recovered.   _____

3. The ancient country Egypt is sometimes called the gift of the Nile.   _____

4. Guam an island in the Pacific Ocean was the site of battles in World War II. _____

5. The Archimedes pump reportedly an invention of Archimedes
   from the third century B.C. was used for irrigation.   _____

6. The boat the *Janice* sports a sign advertising the state of Washington.   _____

7. The Great Lakes the largest freshwater lakes in the world lie on
   northern border of the United States.   _____

CHAPTER 2

Lesson 2 Appositive Phrases

More Practice

A. Identifying Appositive Phrases

Underline the appositive phrase in each sentence. Write the noun it identifies to the right. Then identify each phrase as **E** if it is essential or **NE** if it is nonessential, and add commas where they are needed to set off nonessential phrases.

EXAMPLE The iceberg, <u>a threat to navigation</u>, is the size of New Jersey. *iceberg, NE*

1. The Amazon River the second longest in the world is 4,000 miles in length. _____

2. The book *Life on the Mississippi* chronicles events during the steamboat era. _____

3. Hydroelectric plants facilities that convert water power to electricity generate about one-fourth of the electric power in the world. _____

4. The famous waterfall on the Zambezi Victoria Falls is one of the natural wonders of the world. _____

5. The only water link between the Atlantic and the Great Lakes the St. Lawrence Seaway is used by ships of all nations. _____

6. Antarctic icebergs large pieces of ice from the Antarctic icecap are much larger than those found in the North Atlantic. _____

7. The painter J. M. W. Turner was perhaps best known for his seascapes. _____

8. An island located in the Arctic region Greenland is responsible for the icebergs in the North Atlantic. _____

9. Woody plants typically trees and shrubs grow in swamps or bogs. _____

10. Rudyard Kipling's story "The Elephant's Child" described the Limpopo River in South Africa in a colorful way. _____

B. Using Appositives in Sentences

Choose one of the nouns in each sentence that needs clarification or that can be given extra information. Rewrite the sentence, adding an appositive to the noun you chose. Use commas as necessary.

1. That vase on the table costs $150.

_____

2. For breakfast we had oatmeal and toast with jelly.

_____

3. Two of the boys carried the sofa into the dorm room.

_____

Lesson 2

Appositive Phrases   *Application*

A. Writing with Appositives and Appositive Phrases

Combine each set of sentences into a single sentence by using appositives or
appositive phrases. Use commas as they are needed.

1. Oceans cover about 71 percent of the earth's surface. Oceans are large bodies
   of salt water.

   _____

2. The continental shelf extends toward the sea for about 43 miles. The
   continental shelf is the submerged section of a continent.

   _____

   _____

3. Mid-ocean ridges are located in the central parts of the oceans. Extensive
   mountain ranges in the ocean are called mid-ocean ridges.

   _____

   _____

4. The Mid-Atlantic Ridge and the East Pacific Rise wind across the oceans for
   40,000 miles. The Mid-Atlantic Ridge and the East Pacific Rise are sections of a
   continuous ridge system.

   _____

   _____

B. Using Appositives and Appositive Phrases

You are writing an ad for a new tour company that will operate boat tours on the
Great Lakes, major rivers, and along the coasts of the United States. Choose a
body of water or waterway with which you are familiar. Write one or more
paragraphs describing a tour of that area, the views, and the side trips that
travelers can enjoy. Use at least four appositives or appositive phrases in your
paragraph. After each appositive or appositive phrase, write in parentheses
whether it was essential **(E)** or nonessential **(NE).**

_____

_____

_____

_____

_____

_____

_____

CHAPTER 2

Verbals: Participial Phrases   *Teaching*

A **verbal** is a verb form that acts as a noun, an adjective, or an adverb. A **verbal phrase** consists of a verbal plus its modifiers and complements.

A **participle** is a verbal that acts as an adjective. A **participial phrase** consists of a participle plus its modifiers and complements.

> <u>Ripping free from the lamppost</u>, the banner fluttered to the street. (The participle is *Ripping*.)

> <u>Awakened by the blaring horns</u>, Aaron looked out the window. (The past participle *awakened* modifies *Aaron*.)

An **absolute phrase** consists of a participle and the noun or pronoun it modifies. This phrase has no grammatical connection to the sentence in which it appears, although it provides information for the sentence.

> <u>The bus rumbling away in the distance</u>, we started the long walk home.

Identifying Participial Phrases and Absolute Phrases

Underline once the participle or participial phrase in each sentence. Underline twice the word that the participle or participial phrase modifies. Write **ABS** after the single sentence in which the participle or participial phrase is part of an absolute phrase.

1. Whistling loudly for a cab, Woodrow startled the elderly gentleman. _____

2. The train terminal, built at the turn of the century, was considered an historic treasure. _____

3. At the air show, four thunderbirds flying wing to wing somersaulted across the sky in perfect formation. _____

4. The leaping water in the monumental fountain was a tourist attraction. _____

5. Torn by too many choices, Cecelia decided to take a long walk. _____

6. Chugging slowly against the current, the tugboat left port to meet the freighter. _____

7. Bending down quickly, George scooped the kitten out of the busy street. _____

8. The train having arrived late at the station, many passengers were disgruntled. _____

9. Guided by the delicious aroma, Sam found his way to the bagel shop. _____

10. A stalled car on the freeway caused a huge traffic jam. _____

11. The 10K Turkey Trot, begun as a one-time fund raiser, became an annual event at City Park. _____

12. Climbing to the top of the pole, the electrician worked on the traffic signal. _____

Lesson 3

Verbals: Participial Phrases

More Practice

A. Identifying Participles and Participial Phrases

Underline once the participle or participial phrase in each sentence. Underline twice the word that the participle or participial phrase modifies. Write **ABS** after any sentence in which the participle or participial phrase is part of an absolute phrase.

1. Route 12, known as the shortcut to school, actually takes ten minutes longer than West Boulevard. _____

2. Broadcasting on location, the radio team raised $5,000 for the Children's Museum. _____

3. The subway car roaring through the tunnel, we could barely hear each other. _____

4. Only the most finely ground coffee is served at that specialty shop. _____

5. Carefully trained on radar, the pilot confidently landed the jet in the thick fog. _____

6. A climbing hydrangea added a bright spot of color to the drab building. _____

7. The young boy clutching the coins for his fare, a mother and child boarded the bus. _____

8. Mr. Bales, dragged through five stores by his wife, plopped wearily on the bench. _____

9. The shaken pedestrian shouted after the careless bicyclist. _____

10. Several arriving passengers lost their luggage in the confusion. _____

B. Using Participial Phrases to Combine Sentences

Use participial phrases to combine each set of sentences into one sentence. Use an absolute phrase in the even-numbered items.

EXAMPLE The main bus routes were well covered. We waited only ten minutes.
The main bus routes being well covered, we waited only ten minutes.

1. The mayor was introduced to the gathering. He was warmly received.

_____

2. All trains were filled to capacity. Disappointed passengers demanded refunds.

_____

3. Food vendors were stationed outside the convention center. They did a brisk business.

_____

4. An electrical storm threatened. The parade was postponed until tomorrow.

_____

5. Tourists arrived in droves. They enjoyed the contemporary art exhibit.

_____

CHAPTER 2

Verbals: Participial Phrases

Application

A. Using Participial Phrases to Combine Sentences

Combine each of these pairs of sentences as a single sentence by using participial phrases. In even-numbered items, use a participial phrase as part of an absolute phrase. Use a comma after each participial phrase that begins a sentence.

1. Mega Movie Theater attracted people from across the city. It was filled to capacity nightly.

   _____

   _____

2. Noisy helicopters circled the stadium several times. Some players on the field seemed distracted.

   _____

   _____

3. A tourist tram carried visitors between historical buildings. It was closed due to the snowstorm.

   _____

   _____

4. The short-circuit stopped the hotel elevator. Guests were using the stairs.

   _____

   _____

B. Using Participles and Participial Phrases in Writing

Write a sentence using each of these participial phrases. Use a comma after each phrase that begins a sentence. Use participial phrases within absolute phrases in the even-numbered items.

1. filled with bored commuters _____

   _____

2. having walked seven blocks _____

   _____

3. cruising the harbor _____

   _____

4. being stranded at the terminal _____

   _____

5. rising swiftly to the sky _____

   _____

Name _____ Date _____

Lesson 4

Verbals: Gerund Phrases   *Teaching*

A **gerund** is a verb form, or verbal, that ends in *–ing* and functions as a noun. A **gerund phrase** consists of a gerund plus its modifiers and complements.

    <u>Climbing</u> <u>mountains</u> appeals to many people.

Gerunds and gerund phrases may be used anywhere nouns may be used. To test whether a verbal or phrase is a gerund or gerund phrase, try substituting a noun for it.

As subject	<u>Seeing the grandeur of a mountain</u> makes me feel small.
As predicate nominative	My hobby is <u>photographing mountains</u>.
As direct object	One climber justified <u>climbing a mountain</u> by saying, "It's there."
In apposition	Sir Edmund Hilary's feat, <u>climbing Mount Everest</u>, is still famous.

A. Identifying Gerunds and Gerund Phrases

In each sentence, underline once every gerund phrase. Underline twice each gerund.

1. The ship's captain is usually responsible for navigating a narrow channel.

2. Georges Seurat invented pointillism, painting with small dots.

3. The terms *smelting* and *sintering* relate to metallurgy.

4. An increasingly popular sport is cross-country skiing.

5. Storing data and retrieving archives are two useful computer functions.

6. Meteorologists measure high-altitude temperatures by sending up balloons.

7. Harps and harpsichords require tuning, especially in damp weather.

8. Rhea gave preparing her term paper her full attention for two weeks.

B. Identifying Gerunds and Gerund Phrases

Underline each gerund or gerund phrase. On the blank, write how it is used: **S** for subject, **PN** for predicate nominative, **DO** for direct object, **IO** for indirect object, **OP** for object of a preposition, or **APP** for appositive.

1. The crumbling of Mount Fuji is a serious problem.   _____

2. The Japanese government gave preserving this significant landmark
   much attention.   _____

3. After ten years of studying the problem, the Japanese government
   decided on a possible solution.   _____

4. The Japanese plan was to repair Fuji by building a barrier.   _____

5. Their aim was stopping the constant rock and sand slides.   _____

6. Constructing similar walls has helped in the past.   _____

7. Another benefit, protecting the city of Fujinoyama, was equally desirable.   _____

8. Unfortunately, difficulties arose in bringing workers and supplies to the site.   _____

9. Project managers tried flying supplies in by helicopter.   _____

10. Stopping the decay of Mount Fuji may be impossible.   _____

Lesson 4 Verbals: Gerund Phrases   *More Practice*

A. Identifying Gerunds and Gerund Phrases

Underline each gerund or gerund phrase. In the blank, write how it is used:
S for subject, **PN** for predicate nominative, **DO** for direct object, or **OP** for object
of a preposition.

1. Scaling the highest mountains of the world requires skill, stamina,
   and great endurance.   _____

2. Before attempting the actual climb, the participants engage in
   careful preparation.   _____

3. One important step is mapping the route to be taken.   _____

4. Another consideration is determining the location of a base camp and the
   smaller camps higher up the mountain.   _____

5. The proper equipment is essential in making a safe ascent.   _____

6. Climbers practice handling ropes, pitons, chocks, and other specialized gear. _____

7. Knowing the proper techniques to climb on rock, ice, and snow is vital. _____

8. Dangers include falling into crevasses.   _____

9. Climbing in the rarefied atmosphere causes great fatigue.   _____

10. However, the satisfaction gained from achieving the goal is incomparable. _____

B. Using Gerunds and Gerund Phrases

Use gerund phrases to combine each set of sentences into one sentence.

1. Maggie read the atlas as a child. This activity gave her an extraordinary
   love of travel.

   _____

2. Ian's job was quite a challenge. He restored damaged works of art.

   _____

3. They were determined to paint the widow's home in one day. This was
   their objective.

   _____

4. Mary joined the choir. The reason for this was because she loved to sing.

   _____

5. Debra enjoys one particular hobby. This hobby is to knit colorful sweaters.

   _____

Lesson 4 · # Verbals: Gerund Phrases   *Application*

A. Using Gerunds and Gerund Phrases

Write sentences using the following gerunds and gerund phrases in the sentence parts indicated.

1. finding waterfalls that last only through spring (subject) _____

_____

2. painting a snow-capped peak (direct object) _____

_____

3. climbing past the tree line (predicate nominative) _____

_____

4. hearing a yodeler practicing in the distance (apposition) _____

_____

5. taking precautions against a snow slide (your choice of position) _____

_____

B. Using Gerunds and Gerund Phrases in Writing

Would you enjoy climbing one of the highest mountains in the world, such as Mount Everest? Or do you consider such feats risky or unpleasant? Write a short essay explaining your attitude. Use five or more gerunds in your statement.

_____

_____

_____

_____

_____

_____

_____

_____

_____

_____

_____

CHAPTER 2

Verbals: Infinitive Phrases

Lesson 5

Teaching

An **infinitive** is a verb form that usually begins with the word *to* and acts as a noun, an adjective, or an adverb. An **infinitive phrase** consists of an infinitive plus its complements and modifiers.

As noun	To work outside can be challenging. (subject of sentence)
	Drivers want to avoid construction sites. (direct object)
	The crew's job is to maintain the road. (predicate nominative)
As adverb	To keep workers safe, signs were erected. (tells why erected)
As adjective	Directions to drive more slowly were enforced by police. (tells which directions)

A. Identifying Infinitives and Infinitive Phrases

Underline the infinitive phrase in each sentence. Underline twice the infinitive.

EXAMPLE Weather forecasters work to predict damaging storms.

(1) Reporting from Colorado, Donald Mulcahy stated that this was the third snowstorm to hit the western states this week. **(2)** The central Rockies, already blanketed by snow, were getting ready to dig out again.

(3) "Preparing for a storm is something we're always ready to do here," Mulcahy said. **(4)** "If it isn't snow, it's rain," he added, turning to point on the weather map to southeast Texas. **(5)** Heavy flooding has begun to snarl traffic there. **(6)** "In our area, the power company has asked employees to work around the clock. **(7)** To restore knocked-down power lines will be a big job. **(8)** Other than essential workers, everyone has been asked to stay off the streets. **(9)** That will give snowplow crews a chance to move freely. **(10)** To have traffic back to normal by the end of the week is about the best we can expect."

B. Identifying Infinitive Phrases

Underline the infinitive phrase in each sentence. If the phrase is used as an adjective or adverb, write **ADJ** or **ADV** on the line at the right. If the phrase is used as an noun, write **S, O,** or **PN** to identify whether it is used as a subject, object, or predicate nominative.

1. To repair a downed power line during a storm demands complete concentration. _____

2. The head ranger planned to send a fresh crew to the raging forest fire. _____

3. Lift equipment helps linemen to reach the transformers located on telephone poles. _____

4. The backhoe operator's task was to dig the trench for the new water line. _____

5. To maneuver earth-moving machinery requires great skill. _____

6. Cranes to lift heavy objects have made the construction of tall buildings easier. _____

7. Weary road crews expected to remain on the job until the blizzard was over. _____

8. Skyscrapers under construction have elevators to carry the crew. _____

Lesson 5

Verbals: Infinitive Phrases

More Practice

A. Identifying Infinitive Phrases

Underline the infinitive phrase in each sentence. If the phrase is used as an adjective or adverb, write **ADJ** or **ADV** on the line to the right. If the phrase is used as an noun, write **S, O,** or **PN** to identify whether it is used as a subject, object, or predicate nominative.

1. To go to medical school was an unusual choice for a woman in the 1890s. _____

2. Alice Hamilton, however, decided to become a doctor. _____

3. In 1897, she went to Chicago to teach pathology at Northwestern University. _____

4. She soon discovered there was work to do among the various immigrant groups in Chicago. _____

5. In 1909, a commission to study the relationship between occupations and disease was established in Illinois. _____

6. Dr. Hamilton was asked to be the director of the study. _____

7. She interviewed hundreds of factory workers to establish the causes of lead poisoning. _____

8. In many occupations, as she found, to breathe in the dust is life-threatening. _____

9. Dr. Hamilton also helped to prevent poisoning in nitric acid factories. _____

10. Many measures that have been taken to increase occupational safety owe their beginnings to Dr. Alice Hamilton. _____

B. Using Infinitive Phrases

Use each of the following infinitive phrases in a sentence.

1. to dispose of hazardous waste

_____

2. to use goggles and face masks

_____

3. to check equipment for signs of wear

_____

4. to reduce speed

_____

5. to anticipate potential dangers

_____

Name _____ Date _____

Lesson 5 **Verbals: Infinitive Phrases**   *Application*

A. Using Infinitive Phrases to Combine Sentences

Combine each pair of sentences below, changing one of the sentences into an
infinitive phrase. Add, drop, or change words as needed.

> **EXAMPLE** Highway workers wear bright reflective vests. These vests are easily
> seen by motorists.
>
> **REVISION** *Highway workers wear bright reflective vests to be easily seen
> by motorists.*

1. At a construction site, wearing hard hats is required. It protects wearers from
falling debris.

_____

2. On some jobs, a flagger stands several feet from the work site. The flagger's
job is regulating the flow of traffic.

_____

3. Heavy trucks emit a loud beeping sound when they go in reverse. The noise
warns workers.

_____

4. Steel-toed boots are required on some jobs. They protect the worker's feet in
hazardous areas.

_____

5. Some workers need special headsets if their jobs are noisy. This equipment
minimizes hearing loss.

_____

B. Using Infinitive Phrases

Use each of the following infinitive phrases in a sentence in the function identified
in parentheses.

1. to wear protective clothing (adjective)

_____

2. to observe the change in seasons (predicate nominative)

_____

3. to keep traffic moving (object)

_____

4. to work in all kinds of weather (subject)

_____

5. to keep workers safe (adverb)

_____

Lesson 6

Problems with Phrases   *Teaching*

A **misplaced modifier** is a word or phrase that is placed so far from the word it modifies that the meaning of the sentence is unclear or incorrect.

> EXAMPLE The potatoes are on the stove to be mashed. (Will the stove be mashed?)
> REVISION The potatoes to be mashed are on the stove.

A **dangling modifier** is a word or phrase that does not clearly modify any word in the sentence.

> EXAMPLE Coming home late, the potatoes weren't mashed. (Who came late?)
> REVISION Coming home late, I didn't mash the potatoes.

A. Finding the Words Modified by Misplaced Phrases

Each underlined phrase is misplaced. On the line to the right, write the word that the phrase was intended to modify.

1. Andrew put the clothes into a basket <u>to be washed</u>.   _____

2. Indira left a message concerning a book about mining
   <u>on the refrigerator door</u>.   _____

3. Prehistoric people counted cattle <u>using fingers and thumbs</u>.   _____

4. The plane's passengers glimpsed the ruins of Monde Alban
   <u>landing in Oaxaca</u>.   _____

5. I have difficulty eating foods such as noodles and peas
   <u>with chopsticks</u>.   _____

6. She saw the announcement about a homework assignment
   assigned by Mr. Jackson <u>hanging in the hall</u>.   _____

B. Identifying Misplaced and Dangling Phrases

Underline the misplaced or dangling phrase in each of the following sentences. Then rewrite the sentence, correcting the error. Add or change words as needed.

1. Hidden by the weeds, I didn't see the rabbit.

_____

2. The cat sat there while I poured the milk purring softly.

_____

3. Did you put the new sheets in the guest room on the bed?

_____

4. Melvin heard a song he liked turning on the radio.

_____

5. Riding down in the elevator, my stomach felt as if it had dropped 20 stories.

_____

6. To win this jingle-writing contest, more than luck is needed.

_____

CHAPTER 2

Lesson 6 Problems with Phrases   *More Practice*

Correcting Misplaced and Dangling Phrases

If a sentence contains a misplaced or dangling phrase, rewrite it to eliminate the error. If the sentence is correct, write **Correct**.

1. Exhausted by the long day, sleep was impossible to resist.

_____

2. We saw the dome of Missouri's state capitol entering Jefferson City.

_____

3. Sleeping late after the prom, most of us never noticed the small earthquake.

_____

4. Jeff found cheese, bread, and some eggs looking for something to eat.

_____

5. To be mailed today, I'll spend the morning typing.

_____

6. My dog raced along as I left the house barking loudly.

_____

7. Auden piled the branches to be fed into the chipper in the side yard.

_____

8. Taking another look, the Big Dipper finally became visible.

_____

9. Shirley always wore a bathing cap when she swam on her head.

_____

10. Talking loudly, the phone interrupted her conversation.

_____

11. After a hot day at the beach, a shower sounded inviting.

_____

12. I saw two deer and a raccoon riding my bicycle through the park.

_____

13. Fans at the tournament lined up three hours before the scheduled starting time.

_____

14. Abandoning the dockyards, the island of Malta was left by the British Navy.

_____

Problems with Phrases

Application

A. Correcting Misplaced and Dangling Phrases

If a sentence contains a misplaced or dangling phrase, rewrite it to eliminate the error. If the sentence is correct, write **Correct**.

1. Waving his arms wildly, the dog barked loudly at Eric.

_____

2. Grandma looked at the vase and then at me, cracked in half and lying on the floor.

_____

3. Munching continuously, the cookies disappeared quickly.

_____

4. We stood in the rain watching the chipmunks play under the tree with our umbrellas.

_____

5. To use the grinder correctly, instructions should be followed exactly.

_____

B. Correcting Misplaced and Dangling Phrases in Writing

Rewrite this paragraph, correcting the misplaced or dangling participles.

My great-grandfather Seth fancied himself quite an inventor on my mother's side of the family. As a young man the radio was a new invention. "I can do something with that," he declared emphatically. Seth would talk over his ideas with the cows doing his chores. At night he worked in the barn entangled in wires. Pounding and hammering, the night was filled with loud sounds. Finally, covered with dirt and hay, the barn door opened to reveal a triumphant Seth. Gleaming through the dusty haze, he pointed to his new invention. Seth's cows were the first in Guernsey County to have a "whole-barn" sound system.

_____

_____

_____

_____

_____

_____

_____

_____

Sentence Diagramming

More Practice 1

Complete each diagram with the sentence provided.

A. Prepositional Phrases

Adjective Phrase George Washington Carver was a pioneer in agricultural research.

Adverb Phrase He was born in Missouri in 1864.

B. Appositive Phrases

Carver, an orphan, was raised by Moses and Susan Carver.

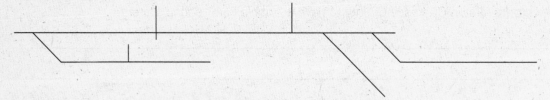

C. Participial Phrases

Present Participle Supporting himself, Carver pursued graduate degrees in agriculture.

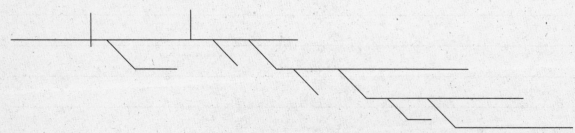

Past Participle In 1896 Carver joined the faculty of the Tuskegee Institute, founded in 1881 by Booker T. Washington.

Sentence Diagramming   *More Practice 2*

D. Gerund Phrases

Gerund Phrase as Subject Improving agricultural methods in the South soon became his chief concern.

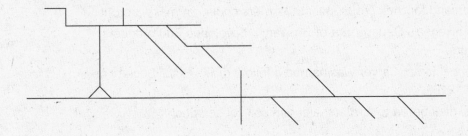

Gerund Phrase as Object of Preposition After 1914, he concentrated on finding hundreds of uses for peanuts.

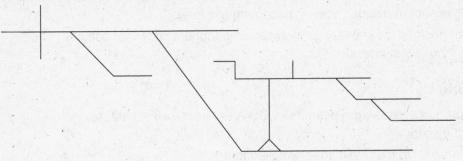

E. Infinitive Phrases

Infinitive Phrase as Adverb Carver worked hard to improve race relations.

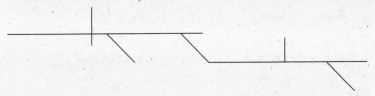

Infinitive Phrase as Noun Carver's goal in his peanut research was to broaden the market for peanut farmers.

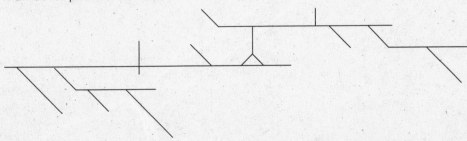

Lesson 7 Sentence Diagramming

Application

On a separate piece of paper, diagram each of the following sentences.

A. Diagramming Prepositional, Appositive, and Participial Phrases

1. Without much demand for their crops, peanut farmers could not make a profit.
2. Carver, head of Tuskegee's Department of Research, developed 300 products made from peanuts.
3. Winning international fame, Carver was named a fellow of the Royal Society of Arts in London in 1916.
4. Carver's bulletins, distributed to farmers, aided in soil conservation.

B. Diagramming Gerund Phrases and Infinitive Phrases

1. Farmers improved their crops by following instructions in Carver's bulletins.
2. Carver began to earn his own living at the age of 11.
3. He had artistic talent but decided against becoming a painter.
4. In 1940, Carver donated his life savings to establish a foundation for agricultural research at Tuskegee Institute.

C. Mixed Practice

1. Some of the products made from peanuts by Carver were a milk substitute, printer's ink, and soap.
2. To call Carver's early life traumatic does not exaggerate.
3. Born a slave, he became an orphan within a year.
4. His mother was stolen by men intending to resell her.
5. After the emancipation of slaves in Missouri in 1865, the toddler George was still raised by his previous owners.
6. Taught to read and write by the Carvers, George determined to continue his education.
7. In 1939, Carver was honored by being awarded the Theodore Roosevelt Medal for his contributions to science.
8. A national monument established in 1951 at Carver's birthplace is one way of showing our appreciation for his work.

Kinds of Clauses
Teaching

A **clause** is a group of words that contains both a subject and a verb. An **independent clause** expresses a complete thought and can stand alone as a sentence.

> The South American <u>rain forests</u> <u>support</u> a diversity of life forms.
>   SUBJECT   VERB

A **subordinate clause,** or **dependent clause,** contains a subject and a verb but does not express a complete thought and cannot stand alone as a sentence.

> When the <u>wind</u> <u>erodes</u> mountains (What happens at this time?)
>   SUBJECT   VERB

A subordinate clause must always be combined with an independent clause.

> <u>When the wind erodes mountains</u>, <u>flat-topped mesas and plateaus are created</u>.
>   SUBORDINATE CLAUSE   INDEPENDENT CLAUSE

Two kinds of words that link or introduce clauses are coordinating conjunctions and subordinating conjunctions. A **coordinating conjunction** joins two independent clauses. Examples of coordinating conjunctions are *and, or, but*, and *yet*.

> The Pacific Ocean is the largest ocean, <u>and</u> Mt. Everest is the highest mountain.
>   COORDINATING
>   CONJUNCTION

A **subordinating conjunction** introduces a subordinate clause.

> <u>Because</u> deserts receive only a little rainfall, they are often covered by sand.
> SUBORDINATING
> CONJUNCTION

The following are some examples of subordinating conjunctions: *after, although, as, because, before, if, in order that, provided, since, so that, until, when, where, wherever, while*.

Identifying Kinds of Clauses and Conjunctions

In each sentence, identify the boldfaced group of words by writing **IND** for an independent clause and **SUB** for a subordinate clause. Then find the conjunction in the sentence. Underline a coordinating conjunction once and a subordinating conjunction twice.

1. Although the oceans appear to be separated, **they are actually joined together.** _____

2. **Before echo sounding was developed,** the depth of the ocean was
measured with weighted lines of hemp or wire. _____

3. The ocean's currents are studied in detail **because they are important to shipping.** _____

4. Whenever Earth's plates slide past one another, **earthquakes can occur.** _____

5. **The North Pole is covered by water,** and the South Pole is covered by land. _____

6. Erupting volcanoes cause great destruction, yet **they also bring many benefits.** _____

7. **As coastal areas become flooded,** the need for wetlands becomes clear. _____

Kinds of Clauses

A. Identifying Conjunctions and Kinds of Clauses

In these sentences, underline once every independent clause, underline twice every conjunction, and place parentheses around every subordinate clause.

1. Although deserts are arid, some cactus plants grow beautiful flowers.
2. The Mississippi River is the longest river in the United States, and the Nile River is the longest river in the world.
3. Underground caves contain amazing sights, yet many people fear their darkness.
4. While it's nearly impossible to live there, many tourists still visit Antarctica.
5. Before the continents separated, Europe and America shared one land mass.
6. A marsh is a wetland with grasses, but a swamp is a wetland with trees.
7. Until the Panama Canal was built, land in Central America separated the two oceans.
8. After it flows for 3,900 miles, the Amazon River empties into the Atlantic Ocean.
9. You may ski in Colorado's mountains, or you may relax in Colorado's hot springs.
10. Hikers should always be physically fit whenever they attempt to climb mountains.

B. Identifying Independent and Subordinate Clauses

Each sentence contains two clauses and a conjunction. Underline the conjunction and write above it either **CC** for coordinating conjunction or **SC** for subordinating conjunction. Above each clause write **IND** for independent or **SUB** for subordinate.

1. Whenever he rides in an airplane, he insists on sitting in the back row.

2. Bears could harass the campground, or rain could make the ground unstable.

3. Wherever her family traveled, they always kept a detailed journal.

4. His cabin had been in the family for 60 years, but Caleb was thinking of selling it.

5. She would not be happy until she soared in a parachute across the canyon.

6. Since everyone else was gone, Robert took the canoe out on the lake alone.

7. Jean intended to swim across the lake unless her parents tried to stop her.

8. After he had been a camper for 30 years, Dan finally saw his first bear in the wild.

Kinds of Clauses

Application

A. Using Clauses in Writing

Use each group of words below in two different sentences. First use it as an independent clause, adding another independent clause either before or after it, and using an appropriate coordinating conjunction. Second, add a subordinating conjunction to the word group and use it as a subordinate clause, joining it to a new independent clause.

1. the ocean is salty

_____

_____

2. earthquakes threaten much of California

_____

_____

3. penguins won't be found at the North Pole

_____

_____

4. they went on an African safari

_____

_____

5. coral reefs support many marine animals

_____

_____

B. Building Sentences with Clauses

Begin with the given sentence. Add to it clauses as described in parentheses. At each step, add the new element to the preceding answer.

Starting Sentence: Many islands look lovely.

1. (Add a conjunction and an independent clause.) _____

_____

2. (Add a conjunction and a subordinate clause.) _____

_____

3. (Add a conjunction and another independent clause.) _____

_____

_____

CHAPTER 3

Adjective and Adverb Clauses

Lesson 2

Teaching

An **adjective clause** is a subordinate clause that modifies a noun or pronoun. Like an adjective, it tells *which one* or *what kind*. An adjective clause may be called a **relative clause,** and the word that introduces it is either a **relative pronoun** or a **relative adverb.** Examples of relative pronouns are *who, whom, whose, that,* and *which.* Relative adverbs include *after, before, when,* and *where.*

> The color <u>that you get by mixing yellow and blue paint</u> is green. (Which color?)

An **essential adjective clause,** as in the example above, provides information that is necessary to identify the noun or pronoun it modifies. A **nonessential clause** provides additional, but not needed, information. Use commas to set off a nonessential clause.

> Turquoise, <u>which is my favorite color,</u> is similar to aqua. (nonessential)

An **adverb clause** is a subordinate clause that modifies a verb, adjective, or adverb. Like an adverb, it tells *where, when, why, how,* or *to what extent.* Adverb clauses are usually introduced by **subordinating conjunctions** such as *before, when, because, since, as, than, if, though, until, so that, as, as if, where, wherever.*

> <u>When</u> <u>white light passes through a prism</u>, a band of colors forms. (*When* does the band of colors form? Modifies verb)

Sometimes words in an adverb clause that repeat or almost repeat words in the main clause are not stated, but only implied. Such clauses are called **elliptical.**

> This red is more intense <u>than</u> <u>that red.</u> (more intense than that red is intense.)

Identifying Adjective and Adverb Clauses

For items 1 through 10, underline the adjective or adverb clause that modifies the boldfaced word(s). For items 11 through 14, underline once the adjective or adverb clause and underline twice the word modified.

1. **Yellow and blue,** which are complementary colors, form white light when combined.

2. **John,** who is a painter, keeps a color wheel on his studio wall.

3. When you mix primary colors, you **produce** secondary colors.

4. The red apple **appeared** dark gray because the room was very dark.

5. You could not **see** the colored rings until he spun the black and white disk.

6. The **discovery** that white light contains all the colors was made by Isaac Newton.

7. **Goethe,** whose fame comes from his poetry, also developed color theories.

8. The **terms** that experts use to describe color are hue, saturation, and lightness.

9. Although dogs see the same objects we do, they cannot **see** colors.

10. Color **photography,** which most people use today, is based on light color theory.

11. You produce new colors whenever you blend groups of colors from the spectrum.

12. People who can see only white, gray, and black are called color blind.

13. Moise has been less sure of his sense of color since he was shown the optical illusion.

14. The object that bends white light into beautiful color is called a prism.

Adjective and Adverb Clauses

More Practice

Lesson 2

A. Identifying Adjective and Adverb Clauses and Introductory Words

In each sentence, underline the adjective or adverb clause once. Underline the word modified twice. Circle the relative pronoun or relative adverb that introduces the adjective clause, or the subordinating conjunction that introduces the adverb clause.

EXAMPLE Harry won (because) he campaigned hard.

1. After you receive your diploma, shake hands with the superintendent.
2. The lute, which was popular during the Renaissance, is now rarely played.
3. We went to the movie theater where the film festival is being held.
4. Yoko executes calligraphy better than the other students.
5. Before the Lincoln penny was minted, our coins did not carry portraits.
6. The violet that survived six years in the kitchen died after a week in my bedroom.
7. Carla, who speaks Chinese, will translate the speech.
8. Brandon is as bright as his older siblings.
9. Degas is the painter whom we associate with pictures of ballet dancers.
10. The traffic department put the Yield sign where the accidents had occurred.

B. Identifying Adjective and Adverb Clauses and Elliptical Clauses

Review the sentences and your answers in Exercise A. Then, on the lines below, write the numbers of all the items that belong in each group named.

1. Adjective clauses _____
2. Adverb clauses _____
3. Adverb clauses that are also elliptical clauses _____

C. Identifying Nonessential Clauses

Underline the adjective clause in each of the following sentences. If the clause is nonessential, insert commas where they are needed.

1. Hue which is an attribute of color is determined by wavelength.
2. Albert Munsell who was a seascape painter created a system of color names.
3. Jerry painted some black signs that were difficult to see at night.
4. Purple is the color that Mandy loves most.
5. James Maxwell whose scientific work is well known made the first color photograph.
6. Steve did his report on optical illusions that make us see color in black-and-white drawings.
7. What is the name of that artist whose paintings feature stairs that go in two directions at once?
8. In synesthesia, a person who hears a sound may visualize a color in response.

CHAPTER 3

Name _____ Date _____

 Lesson 2 # Adjective and Adverb Clauses *Application*

A. Using Adjective and Adverb Clauses to Combine Sentences

Combine each pair of sentences into one sentence by changing one of the pair into an adjective or adverb clause. Use the introductory word given in parentheses. Use commas as needed.

1. Isaac Newton is famous for discovering gravity. He also developed color theories. (Use *who*.)

_____

2. White light passes through a prism. It separates into many colors. (Use *when*.)

_____

3. Red cannot be formed by combining colors. Red is called a primary color. (Use *because*.)

_____

4. Stare at a colored area for 30 seconds. You will see color on a white sheet of paper. (Use *if*.)

_____

5. Aristotle saw that eyes need light to see color. His explanation for this fact was incorrect. (Use *although*.)

_____

6. Yellow is a primary color in paint. Yellow is not a primary color in light. (Use *which*)

_____

B. Using Adjective and Adverb Clauses to Develop Sentences

Rewrite each of the following sentences, adding an adjective clause, an adverb clause, or both types of clauses. Use commas as needed.

1. There are no set rules of color harmony.

_____

2. The prism separates white light into many colored lights.

_____

_____

3. Scientists measure the different wavelengths of light.

_____

_____

4. Brenda became an expert at mixing paint colors.

_____

5. You can produce white light.

_____

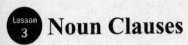

Noun Clauses

Teaching

A **noun clause** is a subordinate clause that is used as a noun. Noun clauses may be used wherever nouns can be used, including as the object of a verbal or as an appositive.

Subject	<u>Whether animals perceive color</u> can be determined.
Direct Object	We know <u>that a cat has excellent night vision</u>.
Indirect Object	They charge <u>whoever uses their binoculars</u> a fee.
Predicate Nominative	His color blindness is <u>what caused the traffic accident</u>.
Object of a Preposition	I'm fascinated by <u>how a fly sees</u>.
Direct Object of Verbal	I'd like to know <u>how its mind deals with all the images</u>.
Appositive	Publish your findings, <u>whatever they may be</u>.

Usually, a noun clause is introduced by one of these words: a **relative pronoun,** such as *what, whatever, who, whoever, whom, whomever,* and *which*; or a **subordinating conjunction,** such as *how, that, when, where, whether,* and *why*.

Identifying Noun Clauses and Their Uses

Underline the noun clause in each sentence. Then underline the initials in parentheses that identify how the noun clause is used: **S** for subject, **DO** for direct object, **IO** for indirect object, **PN** for predicate nominative, **OP** for object of a preposition, **DOV** for direct object of a verbal, or **APP** for an appositive.

1. That yellow is a primary color only in paint did not make sense to me. **(S, PN, APP)**

2. The teacher awarded whoever mixed paint to make green an extra 10 points. **(S, DO, IO)**

3. She understood that the different wavelengths of light produced different colors. **(DO, PN, OP)**

4. Whoever created that color wheel is an excellent artist. **(APP, DOV, S)**

5. We were amazed at how many different colors have been identified. **(OP, DO, PN)**

6. Seeing how a prism split light into colors, John finally understood the concept. **(OP, PN, DOV)**

7. Building a color projector can help you, whoever you are, learn about color and light. **(S, DO, APP)**

8. Optical illusions with afterimages were what she enjoyed the most. **(PN, DO, IO)**

9. He remembered that Albert Munsell created a color system. **(S, PN, DO)**

10. They were bored by how long the speaker talked about color harmony. **(PN, DO, OP)**

11. The position of a color on the color wheel is what determines its complement. **(OP, IO, PN)**

12. The opponent color theory, whatever that is, will be on the test. **(S, APP, IO)**

13. He showed whoever asked to see it his chart of color wavelengths. **(IO, DO, APP)**

14. To see how the students tested for color blindness was the goal of the exercise. **(OP, DOV, S)**

CHAPTER 3

Lesson 3 **Noun Clauses**   *More Practice*

A. Identifying Noun Clauses and Their Uses

Underline the noun clause in each sentence. Then, on the line, write how the noun clause is used: **S** for subject, **DO** for direct object, **IO** for indirect object, **PN** for predicate nominative, **OP** for object of a preposition, **DOV** for direct object of a verbal (gerund, participle, or infinitive) and **APP** for an appositive.

1. The Renaissance was when the countries of Europe rediscovered classical art, literature, and learning.   _____

2. The club sent thank-you notes to our advisors, whoever helped on our project. _____

3. There is absolutely no evidence for what she is alleging.   _____

4. Give whoever requested directions the map of Lantern Lane.   _____

5. Anticipating what questions an interviewer might ask can help you prepare.   _____

6. Do you know why Angles and Saxons invaded the British Isles?   _____

7. Whether or not you succeed depends to a great extent on your attitude.   _____

B. Using Noun Clauses

Use each of the following clauses as a noun clause in an original sentence. In parentheses after your sentence, write how the noun clause is used.

a. whoever mixes red and green paint   d. that our retinas perceive color
b. how much light is in the room   e. whoever studies color theory
c. what terms describe color   f. why green seems restful

1. _____

_____

2. _____

_____

3. _____

_____

4. _____

_____

5. _____

_____

6. _____

_____

CHAPTER 3

Lesson 3

Noun Clauses

Application

A. Using Noun Clauses

Revise this paragraph, replacing each noun clause with a new noun clause that adds new details or changes the story in some way. In parentheses after each revised clause, write how the noun clause is used.

The skill of using color to express personality, whatever that is, is what the lecturer discussed. I took these notes on her speech. Whoever coordinates colors in his or her clothes or room design is immediately recognized as having style. Still, fashion and other trends constantly change what is acceptable or desirable. Many magazines show whoever is interested in personal style different ways to express character through color. Changing where your hair has color streaks may reflect a mood or make a statement. How you use color depends on how you see yourself and show yourself to others.

_____

_____

_____

_____

_____

_____

_____

_____

_____

_____

B. Using Noun Clauses in Writing

You are in charge of the lighting for a children's theater performance of a folk tale. Choose a folk tale that could be dramatized, and describe how you would light the play or some key scene(s). For example, you could describe whether bright or muted lights are used, in which colors, or which characters would be in spotlights. Use at least four noun clauses, and underline them.

_____

_____

_____

_____

_____

CHAPTER 3

Sentence Structure

Teaching

A **simple sentence** has one independent clause and no subordinate clauses. Any part of the sentence, such as subject, predicate, verb, or object, may be compound.

Art and music please adults and children. (compound subject, compound object)

A **compound sentence** has two or more independent clauses joined together. Any of these can be used to join independent clauses: a comma and a coordinating conjunction, a semicolon, or a semicolon followed by a conjunctive adverb.

Museums display art, but they are not the only places with valuable art.

A **complex sentence** has one independent clause and one or more subordinate clauses.

Residents of this community can merely look at nearby walls to find art that reflects the culture of the community.

A **compound-complex sentence** consists of two or more independent clauses and one or more subordinate clauses.

The mural is an ancient art form, but since the 1920s, when Mexican painters began painting murals, modern artists have given it new life.

Identifying Kinds of Sentences

Identify each sentence below with **S** for simple, **CD** for compound, **CX** for complex, or **CC** for compound-complex.

1. Probably the best-known modern muralist is Diego Rivera. _____

2. Rivera's work decorates many public buildings in Mexico City, where people from around the world come just to see his paintings. _____

3. In the 1920s Diego Rivera, José Orozco, David Siqueiros, and other Mexican artists turned to the mural to present the history and legends of their country. _____

4. Rivera drew scenes of life in Mexico before the Spanish arrived. _____

5. Anyone who sees these massive paintings is impressed by their distinctive style, but Rivera also intended to communicate his political beliefs. _____

6. Worldwide, murals are used for political and social purposes because, like advertising billboards, they are seen by so many people. _____

7. The Mexican muralists may be better known, but mural painters were very active in the United States in the first half of the 20th century as well. _____

8. Many of the wall-size works of art in public buildings in the United States date from the 1930s, when artists were working for the Works Progress Administration, or WPA. _____

9. During the Great Depression, the federal government founded the WPA, and it provided work for many artists who would otherwise have left the field. _____

Lesson 4

Sentence Structure

More Practice

A. Identifying Kinds of Sentences

Identify each sentence below with **S** for simple, **CD** for compound, **CX** for complex, or **CC** for compound-complex.

1. A mural is a wall-size work of art, and it can be produced in one of several ways. _____

2. The fastest way to make a mural is by painting on a dry surface, but more enduring murals are made by the *fresco* technique, in which paint is applied to wet plaster. _____

3. Perhaps the most famous muralist of all is Michelangelo. _____

4. Michelangelo used the fresco method when he decorated the ceiling of the Sistine Chapel in the Vatican with scenes from the Old Testament. _____

5. In the fresco method, paint must be applied quickly, before the plaster dries, so the artist prepares by drawing a sketch of what he or she will be painting. _____

6. Mexican muralists such as Diego Rivera and José Clemente Orozco are credited with reviving the fresco technique in modern times. _____

7. Today, the drawing of community murals is promoted by such groups as the Social and Public Art Resource Center, which was founded by Judith Baca and others in Los Angeles in 1976. _____

B. Using Different Kinds of Sentences

Combine each pair of sentences into one sentence of the type indicated in parentheses.

1. Diego Rivera, the Mexican muralist, was married to Frida Kahlo. She was a noted Mexican painter. (complex sentence)

_____

_____

2. Diego Rivera produced murals in Mexico in the 1920s. So did José Clemente Orozco. David Siqueiros also produced murals in Mexico then. (simple sentence)

_____

_____

3. Los Angeles has had many murals painted since the 1960s. It is not the only city in the United States with murals in ethnic neighborhoods. (compound sentence)

_____

_____

4. To create a fresco, first an artist makes full-size drawings on heavy paper. Then the artist or his or her assistants make tracings of the drawings on the plaster. The plaster is still wet. (compound-complex sentence)

_____

_____

CHAPTER 3

Lesson 4

Sentence Structure

Application

A. Using Different Structures to Combine Sentences

Combine the ideas expressed in the simple sentences of this paragraph into only four sentences. In parentheses after each sentence, label what kind of sentence you used.

During the 1960s Hispanic people in the United States wanted to promote appreciation for Hispanic heritage. Many Hispanic artists chose to work with the mural form. The artists knew that young people would see murals as they walked in the neighborhood. The young people would become aware of important people and traditions of the community. They would feel more pride in their background and themselves. Los Angeles has a very large Hispanic population. Artists there formed a committee. It drew in young people to help in creating neighborhood murals. Since then, many impressive murals have been created. Probably the largest of these is the Great Wall of Los Angeles. This mural is half a mile long. It presents the history of California from the viewpoints of women and minorities.

_____

_____

_____

_____

_____

_____

_____

_____

B. Using Different Sentence Structures in Directions

Write a paragraph telling how to produce a work of art or craft, or describing a finished piece. You could write about painting on canvas, working with clay to make a statue or piece of pottery, sewing a quilt, or any other technique with which you have some familiarity. Include at least one of each kind of sentence: simple, compound, complex, and compound-complex. Label in parentheses the sentence type.

_____

_____

_____

_____

_____

_____

_____

CHAPTER 3

Lesson 5 · Fragments and Run-Ons   *Teaching*

A **sentence** must have both a subject and a verb, and express a complete thought.
A **sentence fragment** is only part of a sentence.

A **phrase fragment** is missing both a subject and a verb.

FRAGMENT   <u>In modern days.</u> Women worldwide are gaining more of their rights.
REVISION   In modern days, women are gaining more of their rights.

A **clause fragment** consists of a subordinate clause, which has a subject and verb but does not express a complete thought.

FRAGMENT   <u>Although half their people are women.</u> Some lands limit women's rights.
REVISION   Although half their people are women, some lands limit women's rights.

Other kinds of fragments lack either a subject or a verb.

FRAGMENT   Women in past ages sometimes more respect than modern women.
REVISION   Women in past ages sometimes had more respect than modern women.

A **run-on sentence** is made up of two or more sentences written as if they were one. Often run-ons have a **comma splice,** the incorrect joining of two sentences by a comma. Correct a run-on by separating the sentences or by joining them correctly one of these ways: (1) with a comma and coordinating conjunction; (2) with a semicolon, (3) with a semicolon and conjunctive adverb; (4) by changing one of the sentences into a subordinate clause.

RUN-ON   The role of woman varied from country to country, each land was unique.
REVISION   The role of woman varied from country to country; each land was unique.

Identifying Sentences, Sentence Fragments, and Run-Ons

On the line to the right of each word group below, write **S, F,** or **R** to identify the word group as a complete sentence, a fragment, or a run-on sentence.

1. Geraldine Ferraro ran for vice-president on the Democratic ticket in 1986 she was the first woman to run for this high office.   _____

2. Elizabeth Dole, cutting short her run for the presidency in 1999.   _____

3. Queen Elizabeth I led England into an age of prosperity and international power.   _____

4. In more recent times, with Margaret Thatcher as Prime Minister of Great Britain from 1979 to 1990.   _____

5. Women were rulers in ancient times Queen Hatshepsut of Egypt was sovereign in the land of the pyramids.   _____

6. In Roman times the emperor Julius Caesar confronted another Egyptian queen, Cleopatra.   _____

7. Was known for her beauty as well as her power.   _____

8. During the so-called Dark Ages, which was the period between the fifth and ninth centuries.   _____

9. Women in Europe had more power than you might expect.   _____

10. Some women of that era were wealthy landowners women also had power in the church.   _____

CHAPTER 3

Lesson 5 Fragments and Run-Ons

More Practice

A. Identifying and Correcting Fragments and Run-Ons

On the line after each word group below, write **S, F,** or **R** to identify the word group as a complete sentence, a fragment, or a run-on sentence. Then rewrite any fragment or run-on as one or more correct sentences. Add sentence parts as needed.

1. Is my favorite cartoon character. _____

_____

2. The wood panels were scratched we were staining them. _____

_____

3. Dances, such as the *Deuce Coupe* by Twyla Tharp, have been set to rock-and-roll music. _____

_____

4. The maple seeds spinning like little helicopter blades on their way to the ground. _____

_____

5. Lightning flashed, and rain poured in sheets, we felt safe in the shelter of the lean-to. _____

_____

B. Correcting Fragments and Run-Ons

Rewrite this paragraph, correcting each fragment and run-on. You may add words to any fragment to make it a sentence, or combine it with another sentence. To correct a run-on, you may either separate the sentence or join it correctly.

     The idea of a woman in a position of leadership is not new. Even during the Dark Ages in Europe. Women occasionally held power. The Franks, or French as they were later called, were accustomed to obeying their queens, eventually they followed a woman to war. Joan of Arc led the armies of France. Against the might of England. The English feared her power and her ability to lead eventually she was imprisoned and condemned.

_____

_____

_____

_____

_____

_____

CHAPTER 3

Lesson 5

Fragments and Run-Ons

Application

A. Proofreading for Fragments and Run-Ons

Rewrite this paragraph, correcting each fragment and run-on. You may add words to any fragment to make it a sentence, or combine it with another sentence. To correct a run-on, you may either separate the sentences or join them correctly.

> During the Middle Ages, women often managed great estates and farmlands. A woman did not have to be a great lady to have authority she was often treated as a full partner in a small business, for example. Cloth sellers and cloth makers often husband-and-wife teams. Also trained other family members in the business. In any household the woman's work was of prime importance, she made almost all the goods the family owned.

_____

_____

_____

_____

_____

_____

_____

B. Recognizing and Revising Fragments and Run-Ons

The following is a set of notes to be used in a paragraph about the history of medicine. Translate and rewrite its fragments and run-ons as correct sentences. Add whatever information that you need to make the paragraph understandable.

> We know very little about the infectious diseases. Prevalent before the time of the Greeks. But much about these diseases during the Grecian era. Hippocrates, whose name we associate with the practice of medicine. A Greek. Even before Hippocrates, though, written records were kept. Nature and origin of various diseases. Other evidence, too. For example, that people weren't allowed to bury dead bodies too close to the temple at Delos. Indicates some understanding of how diseases were spread. Hippocrates, though, left detailed records. Inform us about diseases in ancient Greece.

_____

_____

_____

_____

_____

_____

CHAPTER 3

Lesson 6

Sentence Diagramming

More Practice 1

Complete each diagram with the sentence provided.

A. Compound Sentences

You might consider a bed a standard piece of furniture, but it also has been a symbol of wealth.

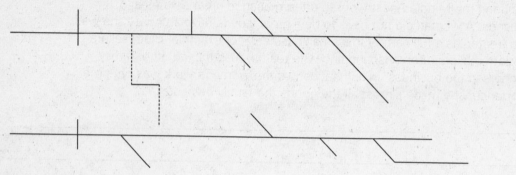

B. Complex Sentences

Adjective Clause Introduced by a Pronoun In ancient times, rich Egyptians slept on low wooden couches that had legs shaped like the legs of animals.

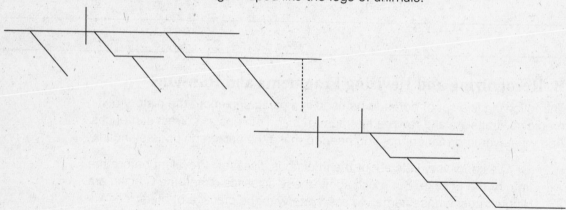

Adjective Clause Introduced by an Adverb In countries where the weather is very hot, people sleep in hammocks.

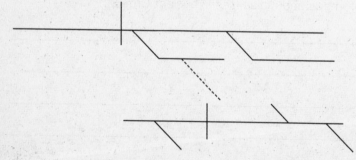

Sentence Diagramming

B. Complex Sentences (continued)

Adverb Clause Before the common people used beds, they slept on pallets on the floor.

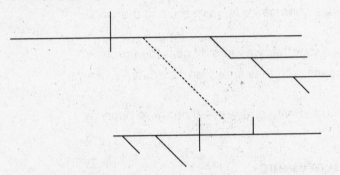

Noun Clause (Used as Subject) That bugs would get into bed with the people was assumed.

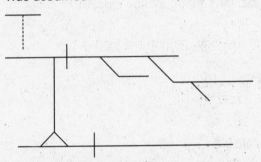

C. Compound-Complex Sentences

Ancient Greeks and Romans lay down while they ate, so they used their beds for dining and sleeping.

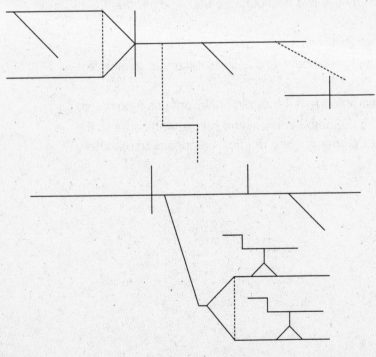

Sentence Diagramming

Lesson 6

Application

On a separate piece of paper, diagram each of the following sentences.

A. Diagramming Compound Sentences and Complex Sentences

1. During the Middle Ages, most European homes had one room, and the whole family slept on the floor of that room.
2. One reason why everyone slept close together was to stay near the fireplace.
3. Rich people slept on elevated bedsteads, and they kept warm by putting curtains around each bed.
4. The mattresses, which were often stuffed with straw, could not have been very comfortable.

B. Diagramming Complex Sentences and Compound-Complex Sentences

1. In some northern countries, beds were in large cabinets that could be closed against the cold, and people slept in sitting position.
2. In countries where nobles competed to stay near the king, getting the king out of bed became a ceremony.
3. Nobles assembled in the king's bedroom before he arose.

C. Mixed Practice

1. A Murphy bed is a bed that can be folded into a closet.
2. Hiding the bed in a closet is useful in a room that is not a full-time bedroom.
3. Often, when people find that they need a bed for a short time, they use a dual-purpose bed.
4. A futon that turns into a couch by day is a dual-purpose bed, and another example is the sleeper sofa.
5. The trundle bed was a bed that children usually used.
6. The trundle bed was a small bed on wheels, and it could roll under a full-size bed when it was not in use.
7. For centuries, sailors slept in hammocks, but they did not invent this type of bed.
8. The first hammocks were used in South America, and sailors who came to the West Indies with Christopher Columbus were the first Europeans to use them.

CHAPTER 3

The Principal Parts of a Verb

Lesson 1

Teaching

A **verb** is a word that shows action or state of being. An **action verb,** such as *think* and *speak*, expresses mental or physical activity. A **linking verb,** such as *be* or *seem*, joins the subject of a sentence with a word or phrase that renames or describes the subject.

Every verb has four principal parts: the present, the present participle, the past, and the past participle. With helping verbs, these four parts make all of the verb's tenses and forms.

PRESENT	PRESENT PARTICIPLE	PAST	PAST PARTICIPLE
charge	(is) charging	charged	(has) charged
buy	(is) buying	bought	(has) bought

The past and past participle of a **regular verb** are created by adding *–d* or *–ed* to the present. Spelling changes are needed in some words, for example, *carry–carried*.

Parts of an **irregular verb** are formed in many ways as show below.

Present	Present	Past	Past Participle
Group 1: Forms of present, past, and past participle are the same	burst cut put spread	burst cut put spread	(has) burst (has) cut (has) put (has) spread
Group 2: Past and past participle are the same	bring fling lend say	brought flung lent said	(has) brought (has) flung (has) lent (has) said
Group 3: Past participle formed by adding *-n* or *-en* to the past	break bear steal swear	broke bore stole swore	(has) broken (has) borne (has) stolen (has) sworn
Group 4: The *i* in the present form changes to *a* in the past and *u* in the past participle	begin drink spring swim	began drank sprang or sprung swam	(has) begun (has) drunk (has) sprung (has) swum
Group 5: The past participle is formed from the present, in many cases by adding *-n* or *-en*	do eat shake go	did ate shook went	(have) done (have) eaten (have) shaken (have) gone

Using Principal Parts of Regular and Irregular Verbs

Complete each sentence by writing the principal part of the verb indicated in parentheses. On the line to the right, write **R** or **I** to indicate whether the verb is regular or irregular.

1. Molly is _____ (look; present participle) for a dish to replace
a broken piece. _____

2. At garage sales, people _____ (put; present) out incomplete
sets of dishes. _____

3. At the garage sale, the owners were (spread; present participle) dishes on a table. _____

4. The sellers (say; past) they would sell a dish to Molly for $15. _____

Lesson 1

The Principal Parts of a Verb

More Practice

A. Using Principal Parts of Regular and Irregular Verbs

Complete each sentence by writing the principal part of the verb indicated in parentheses. On the line to the right, write **R** or **I** to indicate whether the verb is regular or irregular.

1. Last week I _____ (cut; past) my finger, and it hasn't healed yet. _____

2. Our pitcher has just _____ (fling; past participle) the ball to third base. _____

3. When I _____ (lend; past participle) you that book, I expected you to return it. _____

4. Who _____ (bring; past) all those dogs to the park? _____

5. My brother-in-law is _____ (earn; present participle) an excellent salary. _____

6. When the dishwasher _____ (break; past), we washed the dishes by hand. _____

7. Their dog had _____ (steal; past participle) a baseball from a nearby yard. _____

8. Have you _____ (try; past participle) this new cordless phone? _____

9. The gossips reported everything that Miranda _____ (say; past) to George. _____

10. According to the witnesses, nobody had _____ (go; past participle) into the room for over an hour. _____

B. Choosing the Correct Forms of Verbs

Decide which form of each verb given in parentheses is needed—the present participle, the past, or the past participle. Write the correct form on the line.

1. Gracie (lend) her friend some money so she could buy a new sweater. _____

2. My uncle (do) something risky when he bought stock in the struggling company. _____

3. The salesperson is (try) hard to sell me the car. _____

4. The real-estate agent had a hard time selling the house because the water pipes had (spring) a leak. _____

5. When I (exchange) my money at the bank, I got a better exchange rate than I did at the airport. _____

6. Now government officials have (say) that tariffs placed on our goods are too high. _____

7. The company has (ship) its goods overseas for five years now. _____

8. Although the thief had (steal) from the store before, he was caught red-handed by the security chief this time. _____

9. Although the store continually cuts its prices, over the past week it has (cut) its prices more than usual. _____

10. The chairperson's statements (shake) public confidence in the company's stock when she made a speech early yesterday. _____

Lesson 1

The Principal Parts of a Verb

Application

A. Proofreading for the Correct Forms of Verbs

Draw a line through each incorrect verb form in this paragraph. Draw this proofreading symbol ‸ next to the error and, in the spaces between lines of type, write the correct form of the verb.

> **EXAMPLE** The law of supply and demand says that if demand for a product has
> *risen*
> ~~raised the~~ price will rise.

A month ago I begun working at a pet store. The animals that have came
to be my favorites are the fish. Every day, no matter what craziness was
breaking out around them, they swum around peacefully. Whenever I fed
them, I measured and shaked the fish food over the water carefully. I
spreaded the food around so that all the fish ate what they wanted.

One morning I was cleaning the outside of the tank. Just as I started to
spray the window-washing fluid at the glass, a bird pecked one of the balloons
in a display. The balloon bursted, surprising me, and I flang the whole bottle of
cleaner into the water.

B. Using Verb Forms Correctly

Write a paragraph that uses at least six of these verbs and verb phrases. Underline each of the verbs and verb phrases. Make sure all verb forms are used correctly.

was/were beginning	stole	has/have said	come(s)
will have eaten	would have burst	is/are bringing	will be seeing

_____

_____

_____

_____

_____

_____

_____

_____

CHAPTER 4

Verb Tenses

Teaching

A **tense** is a verb form that shows the time of an action or condition. There are three simple tenses and three perfect tenses. The set of forms that express the different tenses of a verb is called the **conjugation** of the verb. Below, only the present tense and present perfect tense of *aim* are fully conjugated.

Simple Tenses

	Singular	Plural
Present Expresses an action as it happens, or that happens regularly, or is generally true. (Also see note below.)		
1st Person	I aim	we aim
2nd Person	you aim	you aim
3rd Person	he/she/it aims	they aim
Past Expresses an action that occurred in the past.		
3rd Person	he/she/it aimed	they aimed
Future Expresses an action that will occur in the future.		
3rd Person	he/she/it will aim	they will aim

Perfect Tenses

	Singular	Plural
Present Perfect Shows than an action was completed at an indefinite time(s) in the past, or started in the past but continues in the present.		
1st Person	I have aimed	we have aimed
2nd Person	you have aimed	you have aimed
3rd Person	he/she/it has aimed	they have aimed
Past Perfect Shows that an action preceded another action in the past.		
3rd Person	he/she/it had aimed	they had aimed
Future Perfect Shows that an action in the future will precede another future action.		
3rd Person	he/she/it will have aimed	they will have aimed

Note: The **historical present tense** describes a past event as if it were happening now (*As the British soldiers trudge back to Boston, the farmers, hidden in the bush, aim at them*).

Using Verb Tenses

Underline the form of the verb that correctly completes the sentence. On the blank, write the tense of the verb.

1. In April 1775, the Americans (fought, had fought) British troops at the battles of Lexington and Concord, the first battles of the American Revolution.   _____

2. Before the first battle, the British (have passed, had passed) the Intolerable Acts.   _____

3. A famous painting (depicts, will depict) George Washington crossing the Delaware.   _____

4. A newspaper headline in September, 1777, could have read, "The British (had captured, have captured) Philadelphia."   _____

5. General Prescott (told, has told) his men not to fire on the British "until you see the whites of their eyes."   _____

6. Before the war began, the British (had believed, have believed) they would win easily.   _____

7. In 1783, two years after the British (had surrendered, have surrendered) at Yorktown, the Treaty of Paris, recognizing American independence, was signed.   _____

Lesson 2

Verb Tenses

More Practice

A. Using Verb Tenses

Underline the form of the verb that correctly completes the sentence. On the blank, write the tense of the verb.

1. By the time Cheryl went to bed, she (finished, had finished) reading *Moby Dick*.   _____

2. When a witness takes the oath, he or she (swears, swore) to speak the truth.   _____

3. Teri couldn't count the number of times she (takes, has taken) pictures of her dog.   _____

4. By this time next year, my brother (will graduate, will have graduated) from college.   _____

5. Yesterday, a bee (stung, has stung) me.   _____

6. When I heard the intruder, I (sprang, have sprung) from my bed.   _____

7. If you take that train, you (will arrive, will have arrived) in Chicago tomorrow.   _____

8. Because of yesterday's rains, the river (has overflowed, had overflowed) its banks today.   _____

9. Analogies (puzzle, puzzled) many students taking aptitude tests.   _____

10. Beginning next Tuesday, Juan (will travel, will have traveled) to Antigua.   _____

B. Correcting Verb Tenses

In each sentence below, change the underlined verb to show the correct order of events. Write the correct verb form on the line to the right

1. For almost 200 years, we recall the founders of our nation each Fourth of July.   _____

2. The city of Boston celebrate Evacuation Day on March 17, the date when British troops evacuated the city.   _____

3. The British evacuated because General Washington place 50 stolen canons from Fort Ticonderoga around the city.   _____

4. Each of the 13 states had considered itself a separate entity before they adopt the Articles of Confederation.   _____

5. By the end of 2007, our country be united under the Constitution for 230 years.   _____

6. Prior to 1760, the British tax the colonists rather lightly.   _____

7. In 1775, patriot Patrick Henry say, "Give me liberty or give me death!"   _____

CHAPTER 4

Verb Tenses

Lesson 2

Application

A. Using Verb Tenses

Rewrite the sentence below four ways, changing the tense of its verb to each tense indicated. Add phrases or clauses as needed to show the correct use of the new verb tense.

SENTENCE I plan my activities.

EXAMPLE (past perfect) *Before I started off on my trip, I had planned my activities for every stop.*

1. (past) _____

_____

2. (present perfect) _____

_____

3. (future) _____

_____

4. (future perfect) _____

_____

B. Correcting Verb Tenses

Revise the underlined verbs in the following paragraph to correct errors and show the proper sequence of events. Write the correct form of the verb above each one.

The Continental Congress already <u>established</u> the Articles of Confederation before the American Revolution ended. The Articles <u>have set</u> up a loose confederation. This arrangement <u>allows</u> each state to keep its sovereign independence. The former colonies, at first, preferred not to be subject to a central government. Several years <u>will pass</u> before the 13 states developed the cooperation needed for adopting the Constitution. Now people <u>will take</u> the Constitution for granted. It is unfortunate that many people <u>forgot</u> the strong debate that took place between the ratification of the Articles of Confederation and the ratification of the Constitution.

Lesson 3 # Progressive and Emphatic Forms   *Teaching*

The **progressive form** of a verb expresses an event in progress. Each of the six tenses has a progressive form.

Progressive Forms

Tense	Shows an event that	Example
Present	**is** in progress	The temperature **is falling** sharply.
Past	**was** in progress	Wind speeds **were rising** all morning.
Future	**will be** in progress	Power crews **will be watching** for downed wires.
Present Perfect	began in the past and is continuing in the present	The weather bureau **has been tracking** the storm for hours.
Past Perfect	was ongoing and was interrupted by another past action	Before buying the newest equipment, the bureau **had been using** less efficient computers.
Future Perfect	will be ongoing and will have taken place by a specified future action	By the end of this year, the local office of the National Weather Service **will have been recording** data about this area for 100 years.

The **emphatic form** of a verb makes the verb more forceful. This form has only two tenses, present and past, made by adding *do* or *did* to the first principal part of the verb.

These gauges **do identify** minute changes in humidity.

Identifying Verb Forms

Underline every verb in the progressive form with one underscore. Underline twice any verb in the emphatic form. On the line to the right, name the form of each underlined verb. (Abbreviate *progressive* as **prog** and *emphatic* as **emph.**)

EXAMPLE   The weather report that I was listening to did forecast snow. *past prog, past emph*

1. People have been trying to forecast the weather for many thousands of years.   _____

2. Before D-Day, Allied commanders had been worrying about the effect of bad weather on the invasion.   _____

3. Even without a definite forecast, General Eisenhower did decide on action.   _____

4. Currently, weather researchers are using a wide range of instruments.   _____

5. By 2020, the United States will have been operating some form of weather service for 150 years.   _____

6. The National Weather Service will be issuing an Emergency Warning once the storm does come close to land.   _____

7. Napoleon's troops had been invading Russia when the cold winter weather forced them to retreat.   _____

8. The Geostationary Operational Environmental Satellite does provide crucial information for weather forecasters.   _____

9. The meteorology class was watching the weather patterns for their extra-credit assignment.   _____

10. Many scientists do believe that the burning of fossil fuels is causing the temperature to rise worldwide.   _____

CHAPTER 4

Lesson 3

Progressive and Emphatic Forms

More Practice

A. Identifying Verb Forms

Underline each progressive and emphatic verb form in the following sentences.
On the line to the right, name the form of each underlined verb.

1. The barometer was falling all afternoon as the storm
   approached.   _____

2. Air molecules are moving constantly, and the measure
   of their speed is called temperature.   _____

3. The greenhouse effect has been occurring on
   Earth for billions of years.   _____

4. The Coriolis Force does affect the winds and currents
   around the earth.   _____

5. The waves had been pounding the beach's breaker wall
   for hours before the waters finally broke through.   _____

6. Although many people believe the Bermuda Triangle
   is a paranormal area, scientists did conclude that
   dangerous weather explains many of its mysteries.   _____

7. The meteorologist says our area will be experiencing
   a patch of strong thunderstorms during the evening.   _____

8. By nightfall, the snow will have been falling for
   eight hours.   _____

9. Dew was forming on the grass during the night
   because the cool air became saturated with water vapor.   _____

10. Balloons have been helping meteorologists
    track and predict weather for decades.   _____

B. Using Verb Forms

Underline the verb form in parentheses that best completes each sentence.

1. The class (will be visiting, will have been visiting) the ship *Constitution* tomorrow.

2. Until we gave up and called a plumber, my mother and I (have been trying, had
   been trying) to repair the faucet for hours.

3. From this summer until next spring, high school seniors (will be applying, will
   apply) to colleges.

4. Next week the school clerk (will be working, will have been working)
   here 30 years.

5. Jason (will be celebrating, will have been celebrating) his election victory soon.

6. Libraries (have been storing, had been storing) information long before
   computers were invented.

7. Several people (are eating, were eating) lunch when the fire alarm sounded.

8. During the last few winters, herds of deer (had been feeding, have been
   feeding) on tree bark.

9. Gerald (comes, has been coming) to the meetings for at least six years.

10. Maureen (will take, will be taking) the bus with you every day from now on.

Progressive and Emphatic Forms

Lesson 3

Application

Using Verb Tenses Effectively

In the following essay, the writer imagines being a historian of the 2100s looking back at the "primitive" weather forecasting methods of the early 2000s. The composition compares our current techniques with the imaginary state of forecasting 100 years in the future. However, because of inaccurate verb use, the essay is difficult to understand. Rewrite it on the lines below, making any changes that will improve the paragraph, giving special attention to verb tenses.

Weather forecasting methods will be improving drastically in the last 100 years. Now, in the 2100s, scientists had been calculating exactly how much precipitation a storm will produce. Until PMP (Precipitation Measurement Program) was invented, meteorologists are predicting precipitation amounts using simple mathematical equations. Amazingly, by the turn of the next century, we have been warning people about tornadoes a whole day in advance for almost 50 years. In the first half of the 2000s, before the Tornado Simulator was invented, tornado watchers will have been risking their lives in order to learn more. In a few years, meteorologists were predicting the weather almost two weeks in advance. Although scientific advances in the 20th and 21st centuries were great, meteorologists of that era have been making accurate forecasts for only two to three days in advance at best.

_____

_____

_____

_____

_____

_____

_____

_____

_____

_____

_____

_____

_____

_____

_____

CHAPTER 4

Active and Passive Voice

Teaching

The **voice** of an action verb indicates whether the subject performs or receives the action.

When the subject of a verb performs the action, the verb is in the **active voice.**

> Traditional poetry **uses** rhyme. (The subject, *poetry,* performs the action.)

When the subject of a verb receives the action, the verb is in the **passive voice.**

> Rhyme **is used** in traditional poetry. (The subject, *rhyme,* receives the action.)

The passive form is often used when the person or thing performing the action is indefinite or unknown. It is formed by using an appropriate form of *be* with the past participle of the main verb.

Identifying Active and Passive Voice

The main verb in each sentence is in boldfaced type. If the performer of the action named by that verb is identified, underline that word or phrase. On the line to the right, write **A** if the verb is in active voice or **P** if it is in passive voice.

> **Sample** This poem **was written** by Gerard Manley Hopkins.   *P*

1. Gerard Manley Hopkins **was born** in England in 1844. _____

2. His poems, such as "The Windhover" and "Pied Beauty," **influenced** 20th-century English poets. _____

3. He **entered** the Jesuit order of Roman Catholicism in his early twenties. _____

4. The poems he had already written **were destroyed.** _____

5. After learning and studying Welsh, he **was inspired** to write poetry again. _____

6. Hopkins **wrote** many of his poems about the natural world. _____

7. His poems **were structured** in a manner quite unlike other poetry of his time. _____

8. His metric technique **is called** "sprung rhythm" because it has an abrupt rhythm rather than a smooth one. _____

9. He **used** internal rhyme and alliteration to portray the uniqueness of natural objects. _____

10. Hopkins **moved** to Ireland where he became a professor at University College. _____

11. He **wrote** a series of poems that are called the "terrible sonnets." _____

12. He **was torn** between the world of senses and his religious vocation. _____

13. For the most part, his poems **were published** posthumously. _____

14. The first edition of his work **was published** in 1918, almost 30 years after his death. _____

CHAPTER 4

Active and Passive Voice

Lesson 4

More Practice

A. Identifying Active and Passive Voice Verbs

Underline the main verb in each sentence. On the line to the right, label the verb **A** for active voice or **P** for passive voice.

1. Vanessa writes a poetry column for a literary magazine.   _____

2. Her columns have been printed regularly for the last three years.   _____

3. Young poets have been interviewed for the columns.   _____

4. The column has featured her delightful sense of humor.   _____

5. Besides poems from new writers, she especially likes Hispanic poetry.   _____

6. Her audience is alerted to programs featuring poets as speakers.   _____

B. Identifying and Changing the Voice of Verbs

If a sentence is in the active voice, rewrite the sentence, changing the verb to passive voice. If a sentence is in the passive voice, decide whether the passive construction is better than the active would be. If it is better in passive, write **Correct as is** on the blank line. If it is not, rewrite the sentence in the active voice.

EXAMPLE Cotton Mather praised Anne Bradstreet's poetry.
Anne Bradstreet's poetry was praised by Cotton Mather.

1. The American poet Anne Bradstreet published only one book in her lifetime.

_____

2. In fact, the manuscript was taken without her knowledge by her brother-in-law.

_____

3. He took the manuscript from Massachusetts to a publisher in London.

_____

4. Bradstreet was born in England, probably in 1612.

_____

5. Eight children were raised by her in the newly founded Massachusetts colony.

_____

6. Her feelings about her Massachusetts house burning down are described in one of her well-known poems.

_____

_____

7. Another famous poem expresses her great love for her husband.

_____

CHAPTER 4

Lesson 4 Active and Passive Voice

Application

A. Revising to Avoid Passive Voice

Revise this paragraph, changing verbs from passive to active voice where appropriate.

William Cullen Bryant was born in 1794 in Cummington, Massachusetts. "Thanatopsis," his most famous poem, was written when he was 16 years old. His first volume, *Poems*, was published when he was only 27 years old. The poem "To a Waterfowl," was included in this volume. His poems were written about nature, like the poems of the English poet William Wordsworth. The Berkshire Hills in western Massachusetts were beautifully described by him in several of his poems. The abolition of slavery had been supported by him well before the outbreak of the Civil War.

_____

_____

_____

_____

_____

_____

_____

B. Using Active and Passive Voice

Choose a work of poetry that you are familiar with and enjoy. It may be a lyric poem, a humorous poem, an excerpt from a play written in poetry (such as a speech from one of Shakespeare's works), or any other form of poem, rhymed or not. Write a brief essay explaining why you enjoy the poem. In your essay, use active voice and passive voice verbs in roughly equal numbers.

_____

_____

_____

_____

_____

_____

_____

_____

_____

The Moods of Verbs

Lesson 5

The **mood** of a verb indicates the status of the action or condition it describes. Some actions and conditions are factual, while others exist only as possibilities or ideas.

Indicative mood is used to make statements and ask questions about factual actions and conditions.

STATEMENT   Variety shows were popular in the early days of television.
QUESTION   Were ventriloquists more popular than acrobats?

Imperative mood is used to give a command or make a request. The understood subject in a command is *you*.

COMMAND   Pick a flower from this bunch.

Subjunctive mood is used primarily to express a wish or to refer to actions or conditions that are contrary to fact. The subjunctive form of a verb matches the past form of that verb. The subjunctive form of *be* is *were*.

If a variety show **were** popular now, I might appear as a juggler.

Another subjunctive form is used in formal writing to refer to a request or command.

The top-rated singer insisted that we **give** him a better dressing room.

A. Identifying the Mood of a Verb

Indicate the mood of each underlined verb by labeling it with **IND** for indicative, **IMP** for imperative, or **SUBJ** for subjunctive.

1. <u>Call</u> your parents when you will be late.   _____

2. Harry Truman <u>became</u> president after the death of Franklin
   Delano Roosevelt.   _____

3. <u>Take</u> a moment to look over your term paper before you pass it in. _____

4. The Faculty Advisor urges that the meetings <u>be</u> over by 3:30.   _____

5. <u>Did</u> the aerobics class <u>learn</u> any new dances yesterday?   _____

6. If the school <u>were</u> larger, it could offer a wider variety of classes. _____

7. The ice-skating rink <u>opened</u> last year, and it is the largest in the state. _____

8. Please <u>practice</u> the new songs your clarinet instructor assigned you. _____

9. I wish that the caterer <u>had made</u> two chocolate cakes.   _____

B. Using Subjunctive Mood

Underline the correct form of each verb in parentheses

1. If you (was, were) to appear on a variety show, what skill would you display?
2. My manager would demand that I (be, am) paid very well, whatever I did.
3. What variety show (was, were) most popular around 1950?
4. Since shows were broadcast live, it was necessary that every act (end, ends) exactly on schedule.
5. How would you feel if the camera (was, were) turned off in the middle of your act?

CHAPTER 4

The Moods of Verbs

More Practice

A. Changing the Mood of a Verb

On the line to the right, identify the mood of the underlined verb by writing **IND,** **IMP,** or **SUBJ** for indicative, imperative, or subjunctive. Then rewrite the sentence according to the directions in parentheses. Change verb tenses and add or delete words as needed.

1. <u>Will</u> you <u>stop</u> at the traffic lights? (Change to imperative mood.)

_____

2. My little sister thinks that her doll <u>is</u> alive. (Change to subjunctive mood.)

_____

3. Mother asked that we <u>mow</u> the lawn. (Change to indicative mood.)

_____

4. You <u>will have sat</u> here for one hour. (Change to imperative mood.)

_____

5. <u>Is</u> this a magic carpet? If so, we could fly to an enchanted island. (Change to subjunctive mood.)

_____

6. The sign at the roller coaster says, "<u>Stay</u> in your seat till the ride stops!" (Change to subjunctive mood.)

_____

B. Using the Correct Mood of a Verb

Underline the correct form of the verb. On the line to the right, indicate which mood you used. Write **IND** for indicative, **IMP** for imperative, or **SUBJ** for subjunctive mood.

1. When a reporter appears on television, he or she (wear, wears) make-up.

2. If I (was, were) an actress, I would prefer to act on a prime-time series rather than a daytime series.

3. Please (teach, teaches) me how to use the sophisticated camera.

4. If Kyle (were, was) older, he could be a participant on our favorite game show.

5. When a newscaster (make, makes) a mistake, is that speech retaped?

6. "(Wait, Waits) in line if you want to be a member of the studio audience," ordered the producer.

7. I (was, were) walking up the ramp when a reporter stopped me to ask questions.

8. The talk show host requested that the guests (be, are) introduced to her before the show began.

CHAPTER 4

The Moods of Verbs   *Application*

A. Using the Correct Mood

Imagine that all the game shows on television joined forces and held a competition to choose contestants. To be invited onto a show, you must write a short essay explaining why you want to appear on that show and what you think you would do as a guest there. Write your application below. Include in your passage at least two verbs in the indicative mood, at least two in the imperative mood, and at least two in the subjunctive mood. After each verb, write **IND, IMP,** or **SUBJ** in parentheses to identify its mood.

_____

_____

_____

_____

_____

_____

_____

B. Proofreading for Correct Mood

Below is an application for the contest described in Exercise A, but it fails to follow the directions completely, and it includes several errors in verb moods. Revise the passage to include verbs in the moods described in the above directions, used correctly. Write the correct verb above any incorrect verb.

   If I was (IND) a contestant on the show "Leapfrog," I would be the

quickest jumper to compete. You tell (IMP) me to hop and crawl down the line

of contestants, and you will find me to be the best entertainment for the

audience. I be practicing (SUBJ) the game of Leapfrog every day since I was a

young child. In addition, I insist that no prizes are (IND) awarded to me since I

will gain enough satisfaction from competing in my favorite game on national

television. Were (SUBJ) the last winner you had as talented as I am? No! I

think you should pick (IMP) me because it has always been my dream to

amaze the audience with my leaping and crawling abilities.

Problems with Verbs   *Teaching*

Improper Shifts in Tense An **improper shift** is the use of different tenses to describe two or more actions that occur at the same time. Avoid problems by using the same tense to express two or more actions that occur at the same time. Use different verb tenses and forms to show how events are related in time or to emphasize them differently.

> We **examined** the Escher picture while we **waited** for you.
> Even after we **had examined** the picture, it **confused** us.

Confusing Verbs Avoid using the wrong verb in these pairs of similar verbs:

lie, lay, (has) lain	to rest in a flat position	**leave,** left, (has) left	to allow to remain
lay, laid, (has) laid	to place	**let,** let, (has) let	to permit
rise, rose, (has) risen	to go upward	**bring,** brought, (has) brought	to carry toward
raise, raised, (has) raised	to lift	**take,** took, (has) taken	to carry away from
sit, sat, (has) sat	to occupy a seat		
set, set, (has) set	to put or place		

Incorrect Use of *Would Have* Do not use *would have* in *if* clauses when the past perfect tense is needed to express the earlier of two past actions.

> INCORRECT If I would have built his steps, I could have gone up and down at the same time.
> CORRECT If I had built his steps, I could have gone up and down at once the same time.

Misuse of *Would of, Should of, Could of,* or *Might of* Do not confuse these phrases with the verb phrases *would have, should have, could have,* and *might have.*

> INCORRECT I never knew anything could of been so confusing visually.
> CORRECT I never knew anything could have been so confusing visually.

Avoiding Problems with Verbs

Underline the correct verb in parentheses.

1. I (might of, might have) (lain, laid) down on the magician's table but I was shy.
2. When the magician (rose, raised) his hand, I (see, saw) the magic string.
3. If I (had, would have) looked more closely, I could have seen the trick.
4. Gretchen (thought, thinks) she sees the way out of the mirror maze.
5. If I (would have, had) (left, let) my brother participate in the magic trick, he could have appeared on national television.
6. Tommy (set, sit) the hat on the table for the magician to finish his trick.
7. Heather (could have, could of) seen a mirage when we were driving yesterday.
8. If the assistant (took, brought) the key with her when she (left, let) the stage, how did the magician escape from the box?
9. Pablo (should of, should have) (laid, lain) the tickets for the show in a better place.
10. It seemed as though the magician's hat (raised, rose) off the ground.
11. Andrea (has taken, has brought) her juggling pins to this birthday party.
12. My family (will see, had seen) a show when we go to Las Vegas next month.
13. We (sat, set) in our seats only a few moments before the show began.
14. Before she (raised, rose) her glass in the air, the liquid inside the glass had disappeared.

Lesson 6

Problems with Verbs

More Practice

A. Correcting Misused Tenses and Confused Verbs

Underline any error in verb usage in the following sentences. Write the proper verb on the line. If all verb forms in a sentence are correct, write **Correct.**

1. My sister Helena took her CD collection with her to college. _____

2. We set down after the usher brought us to our places. _____

3. The umpire had seen the previous play, but he makes the wrong call. _____

4. Fanny lay her new suit on her bed after she had finished ironing it. _____

5. We all raised our glasses to toast the bride and groom. _____

6. If I had gone to bed earlier, I could of gotten up on time this morning. _____

7. Our dog always lays in a funny position when he sleeps. _____

8. After I had sat the new dishes in the cabinet, the earthquake began. _____

9. Tim should of listened to the advice of his friends. _____

10. After their big party, Mr. and Mrs. Doxer let the house in a mess to take their nightly walk. _____

11. Erika finished her homework while she listens to her new CD. _____

12. Katherine laid down on the couch to watch her favorite movie on television. _____

B. Correcting Misused Tenses

Six sentences in this passage contain incorrectly used verbs. On the lines below, write the numbers of the sentences with errors, and the correct forms of the misused verbs.

(1) Yesterday, I saw an optical illusion that tricks me. (2) In the illusion, two people are standing in opposite corners of a room. (3) Compared to the first person, the other person in the room might of been a giant. (4) If you would have seen this picture, you could never have guessed the truth.

(5) In reality, the floor of the room raises while the ceiling slopes downwards. (6) The artist left the back wall slant forwards as well. (7) The two people are actually the same height. (8) But because the room is uneven, the person in the smaller end seems to be a giant. (9) This type of room is called an Ames Room after the ophthalmologist Adelbert Ames who first built it in the 1940s. (10) The inventor should of seen how surprised I was when I recognized the trick.

_____   _____

_____   _____

_____   _____

Lesson 6 **Problems with Verbs** *Application*

A. Correcting Verb Errors

Underline any verb that is incorrect and write the correct verb or verb form on the line to the right. If the tenses and verb choice need no correction, write **Correct.**

1. Preparing for the party, my godmother sat the placemats on the dining room table. _____

2. Joseph laid the stack of books he had just bought on his school desk. _____

3. When you come to see me this summer, be sure that you take your yearbook. _____

4. Every Friday, the teacher leaves her students eat their breakfasts during first period. _____

5. I could of played in the championship tennis match if I had brought my sneakers. _____

6. After she shook the soda bottle, all the bubbles raised to the top. _____

B. Correcting Problems with Tenses

In the passage below, some of the sentences have incorrect shifts in tense, verbs in the wrong tense, or wrong verbs. Rewrite the paragraph below, correcting ten errors.

> After writing to his cousin in New York, Alexander let London for his first trip to the United States. He plans to fill every day of the six weeks with activities. As sometimes happens, however, his plans go awry. As he have stepped off the plane onto the runway, he twisted his ankle. There he was, laying on the pavement. Cousin Leonard, who was waiting for more than two hours for the plane to land, rushes to his side.
>
> "That's what I call making a three-point landing," Leonard says, trying to smooth things over with a joke as he helped his cousin to raise.
>
> Alexander smiled back bravely. "I just flew in from London," he quipped, "and, boy, were my arms tired."

_____

_____

_____

_____

_____

_____

_____

_____

_____

_____

Name _____ Date _____

Agreement in Person and Number

Lesson 1

A verb must agree with its subject in person and number. Singular subjects take singular verbs; plural subjects take plural verbs. In the present tense of all verbs except *be*, the only form that changes is third person singular. For most verbs, add –*s* to make that form.

	Verbs Other than *Be*		*Be*, Present Tense		*Be*, Past Tense	
	Singular	Plural	Singular	Plural	Singular	Plural
1st	I ride	we ride	I am	we are	I was	we were
2nd	you ride	you ride	you are	you are	you were	you were
3rd	he/she/it rides	they ride	he/she/it is	they are	he/she/it was	they were

Don't be distracted by words that come between the subject and verb.

The **passengers** on the 10:20 A.M. train **are departing** the train at this moment.

A. Identifying Subjects and Verbs That Agree in Number

In each sentence, underline the subject and the verb. On the line following the sentence, write whether the two parts of the sentence **Agree** or **Disagree** in number.

1. A public transportation system relieve traffic congestion. _____

2. The subway systems in many cities are complicated networks of tunnels. _____

3. Workers and shoppers in the city appreciates the speed of a subway. _____

4. Boston were the first city in the United States to have a subway. _____

5. The cost of riding most subways is less than parking fees
   in the downtown area. _____

6. Commuters in Washington, D.C., is pleased with the city's
   modern subway system. _____

B. Making Subjects and Verbs Agree in Number

In each sentence, underline the verb in parentheses that agrees with the subject.

1. The subway in New York City (is, are) one of the largest in the world.

2. All of the cars on each train (is, are) filled during the rush hours.

3. The many lines in this system (carry, carries) commuters all over the city.

4. To many visitors, the trains in New York's system (is, are) unbelievably crowded.

5. The first section of New York's subway system (was, were) opened in 1904.

6. On the west coast, the Bay Area Rapid Transit, called BART, (connect,
   connects) San Francisco with neighboring cities.

7. Subway riders heading east out of the city (travel, travels) under the
   San Francisco Bay.

8. Many other large cities of the world (has, have) subway systems also.

9. Subways in Moscow (has, have) chandeliers and oil paintings.

10. The people of London (call, calls) their subway system "the tube."

GRAMMAR, USAGE, AND MECHANICS WORKBOOK **97**

CHAPTER 5

Agreement in Person and Number

More Practice

A. Making Subjects and Verbs Agree in Number

In each sentence, underline the verb in parentheses that agrees with the subject.

1. Our mascot, as well as the team and coach, (travel, travels) to all of the games.
2. The giraffe's long neck, like the pelican's beak and the crane's long legs, (has, have) been important in the animal's evolution.
3. Three rivers—the Mississippi, Missouri, and Illinois—(meet, meets) in St. Louis.
4. Many words in English (come, comes) from words in other languages.
5. Branwell Brontë, as well as his famous sisters, (was, were) an imaginative writer.
6. We all (need, needs) encouragement and recognition for our efforts.
7. Nurses in the burn unit (know, knows) that patients need emotional support.
8. Emus, flightless birds of Australia, (weigh, weighs) about 100 pounds each.
9. Trips around the world on a freighter (is, are) becoming quite popular.
10. I, together with my cousin, (plan, plans) to attend summer school.
11. The birth of conjoined twins (is, are) a relatively rare event.
12. The needles on a fir tree (is, are) actually its leaves.

B. Correcting Agreement Errors

Underline the six verbs in this paragraph that do not agree with their subjects. On the lines below, write the numbers of the sentences in which you find agreement errors. After each sentence number, write the subject and the verb form that agrees with it.

(1) The subway trains in Washington, D.C., is called the Metro. (2) The Metro links Washington, D.C., Maryland, and Virginia with more than 90 miles of railway and over 400 Metrobus routes. (3) Each passenger riding the trains need to buy a farecard. (4) Farecard machines at the entrances of each station sells farecards and special passes for a variety of prices. (5) This way commuters to the city use the same farecard every day. (6). The Metro, along with all the Metrobuses, carry about 900,000 riders daily. (7) Metro passengers who must take a Metrobus can obtain a bus transfer for only 25 cents. (8) The five distinct lines in the Metro are named by color and by their final destinations. (9) The police force in the Metro stations monitor the activities to ensure that the Metro is one of the safest public transportation systems in the world. (10) The Metro, unlike other public transportation systems, prohibit eating, drinking, and smoking on the trains to keep them clean.

_____   _____

_____   _____

_____   _____

Lesson 1

Agreement in Person and Number   *Application*

A. Proofreading for Errors in Agreement

Find the verbs in this paragraph that disagree with their subjects. On the lines below, rewrite the paragraph, correcting all agreement errors.

One of the greatest engineering feats of the 20th century are the tunnel under the English Channel. The idea of a tunnel between two countries are about 200 years old. However, lack of technology, funding, and interest delayed the project until 1987. The tunnel between Cheriton, England, and Calais, France, which opened in 1994, are called the Chunnel. The trains under the sea travels at 80 miles per hour. The capacity of the tunnels are 600 trains per day. Actually, three tunnels exist under the Channel. One of the tunnels are a service tunnel. Under the water, the tracks runs for 24 miles. The trip takes only 35 minutes.

_____

_____

_____

_____

_____

_____

_____

_____

_____

B. Making Subjects and Verb Agree in Writing

Choose one of the topics below and write a paragraph of at least five sentences about it. Use the present tense throughout. Make sure the subjects and verbs of all the sentences agree.

Why public transportation is a good idea
San Francisco cable cars (or another old transportation system)
Why I like (or dislike) using public transportation
Ideas for improvement in public transportation in my area

_____

_____

_____

_____

_____

_____

_____

_____

CHAPTER 5

Name _____ Date _____

Indefinite Pronouns as Subjects   *Teaching*

When used as subjects, some indefinite pronouns are always singular and some are always plural. Others can be singular or plural depending on how they are used.

Indefinite Pronouns

Always Singular					Always Plural	Singular or Plural	
another	each	everything	no one	someone	both	all	most
anybody	either	much	nothing	something	few	any	none
anyone	everybody	neither	one		many	more	some
anything	everyone	nobody	somebody		several		

<u>Each</u> of our watches **shows** a different time.

<u>Several</u> of our watches **are** ten minutes ahead of the others.

<u>All</u> of our <u>plans</u> **depend** on coordination. (There are many plans.)

<u>All</u> of our <u>timing</u> **is** going haywire. (The timing is considered as one quantity.)

A. Identifying Indefinite Pronouns

In each sentence, underline the indefinite pronoun subject and the verb. On the line, label the subject as **Singular** or **Plural.** If the pronoun can be either singular or plural, draw two lines under the word naming the person(s) or thing(s) it refers to.

EXAMPLE <u>Some</u> of the <u>planning</u> <u>was completed</u> a month ago.   *Singular*

<u>Some</u> of the <u>plans</u> <u>were copied</u> from an earlier project.   *Plural*

1. None of the runners are nationally known. _____

2. Most of the race is uphill. _____

3. Several of the best runners have not shown up. _____

4. Some of the spectators have run onto the track. _____

5. All of the judges' watches were synchronized. _____

6. None of the track is free of debris. _____

B. Making Indefinite Pronouns and Verbs Agree

In each sentence, underline the indefinite pronoun used as the subject. Then underline the verb form in parentheses that agrees with the subject.

1. Nobody among the runners (was, were) penalized due to the defective clock.

2. Neither of the winners, male or female, (was, were) affected.

3. Several of the slower runners (is, are) filing a complaint.

4. Most of the judges (think, thinks) the results were accurate.

5. Few of the races that I've run in (have, has) reported accurate results except for the winners.

6. Some of the complaints (were, was) bizarre.

7. But no one (was, were) complaining about the food and drinks afterwards.

8. Anything out of the ordinary affecting a race always (cause, causes) controversy.

9. One of the runners (was, were) saying that all the ruckus made it more fun.

Indefinite Pronouns as Subjects

A. Making Verbs Agree with Indefinite Pronoun Subjects

In each sentence, underline the indefinite pronoun used as the subject. Also underline the verb. If the verb agrees with the subject, write **Correct** in the blank. If it does not agree, write the correct verb in the blank.

1. Anybody interested in police work needs to pass a comprehensive exam. _____

2. Some of the songs by Irving Berlin has become classics. _____

3. According to the magazine article, one of those stars are a supernova. _____

4. Neither of the islands have been inhabited for years. _____

5. Many of the flowers in Hawaiian tourist hotels have been imported. _____

6. Somebody able to speak two languages fluently are bilingual. _____

7. Most of the teas come from China, India, and Japan. _____

8. None of the astronomers knows much about the new space telescopes. _____

9. Everything in the exhibit of Egyptian sculptures were fascinating. _____

10. Most of the glaciers in Europe is in the French and Swiss Alps. _____

11. Either of these encyclopedias give information about the Tony Award. _____

12. Each of the candidates was well qualified to run for governor. _____

B. Using Verbs with Indefinite Pronoun Subjects

For each numbered sentence, write the correct present tense form of the verb on the appropriate line.

If football is a game of inches, running is a game of seconds and split seconds. **(1)** Everything (depend) on the accuracy and precision of the timing. **(2)** But nobody really (believe) in numbers that are in hundredths of a second. **(3)** Anybody who has ever operated a stopwatch (know) it takes a few hundredths just to push the button. **(4)** And do you suppose all of the officials (have) the same reaction time? **(5)** Some of the officials no longer (have) to rely on their reactions. **(6)** Several of the more important races now (use) electronic sensors at the starting and finish lines. **(7)** But all of the others (rely) on the fallible eye and perhaps slow thumb of a human race official.

1. _____   5. _____

2. _____   6. _____

3. _____   7. _____

4. _____

Lesson 2 Indefinite Pronouns as Subjects

Application

A. Checking Agreement of Verbs with Indefinite Pronoun Subjects

Proofread this paragraph for errors in subject-verb agreement. Underscore any verb that does not agree with its subject.

    Not everyone with a large accumulation of objects are a collector. A few of the real collectors, with luck and skill, has gathered objects worth a fortune. Most of the collectors, though, pursue their hobby for fun. Anybody with an interest in this pastime needs space to house a collection. Nearly everything in the world—buttons, posters, glass, china, records, clocks, rocks—have been collected by someone. Some of these things are easier to store and display than others. Most of a collection of buttons, for example, fit easily into a box. On the other hand, very few of someone's antique cars fit into one garage. Both of these items has proved rewarding to collect. Each of the items possess a value to the collector beyond its monetary worth.

B. Using Verbs Correctly with Indefinite Pronouns as Subjects

Do you have a collection? If so, what do you collect? If not, might you collect something in the future, or do you intentionally avoid starting a collection? Write a paragraph or more about your collection or your opinions on collecting. Use at least five of the phrases below as subjects of sentences. You may use the phrases in any order and write additional sentences as well. Make sure each verb is in the present tense and agrees with its subject.

Any of the things	Few of the objects
Either of the sources	Most of the fun
All of the money	Some of the collectors

_____

_____

_____

_____

_____

_____

_____

_____

_____

_____

CHAPTER 5

Lesson 3 **Compound Subjects** *Teaching*

A **compound subject** is made up of two or more subjects joined by a conjunction. A compound subject whose subjects are joined by *and* usually requires a plural verb.

> <u>Blueberries</u> and <u>strawberries</u> **ripen** in different seasons.

Compound subjects that function as a single unit take singular verbs. Also, compound subjects preceded by *each, every*, or *many a* take singular verbs.

> <u>Strawberries and cream</u> **is** a favorite summer dessert.

> Every <u>basket</u> and <u>box</u> **is** filled with berries.

When the parts of a compound subject are joined by *or* or *nor*, the verb should agree with the part closest to it.

> **Is** a <u>trowel</u> or <u>gloves</u> in the bag? Either a <u>trowel</u> or <u>gloves</u> **are** weighing it down.

Making Verbs Agree with Compound Subjects

In each sentence, (1) first decide whether the compound subject is a special case. Do the two parts function as one unit? Or does *each, every*, or *many a* appear before the compound subject? Then underline both parts and the connecting word with one line. (2) If neither of these situations is true, underline each part of the compound subject separately and underline twice the conjunction joining the parts. Finally, underline the correct verb.

> **EXAMPLES** <u>Ham and eggs</u> (<u>is</u>, are) Glenn's favorite breakfast.
> Neither <u>ham</u> <u>nor</u> eggs (was, <u>were</u>) available at the campground.

1. The beach or the forest preserve (is, are) a good place for a picnic.
2. The sounds from the swimming pool and the scent of the honeysuckle (is, are) signs of summer.
3. Oats and barley (grow, grows) well in sandy soil.
4. Many a careless driver and pedestrian (has, have) been responsible for a serious accident.
5. Neither the actors nor the director (has, have) been hired.
6. The fire blazing in the fireplace and the cat sleeping in front of it (make, makes) a charming scene.
7. Chicken and dumplings (taste, tastes) good on a cold evening.
8. Once bitter enemies, the Serbians and the Croatians (was, were) forced to become fellow citizens when Yugoslavia was created.
9. Each hour and minute of this day (has, have) been spent thinking of my ill friend.
10. Neither Prince Andrew nor his younger brother (expects, expect) to inherit the British throne.
11. Crows cawing in a withered tree and scudding gray clouds (was, were) making me uncomfortable.
12. The doctor or the nurses (check, checks) the vital signs of each patient.
13. Every director and actor in the Milburn Dramatic Society (has, have) a role in the forthcoming series of plays.
14. (Is, Are) spaghetti and meatballs on the menu tonight?

CHAPTER 5

Lesson 3 # Compound Subjects

More Practice

A. Using the Correct Verb with a Compound Subject

Write the correct form of the given verb. Make it agree with the compound subject.

1. Neither the ostrich nor the emu (be) able to fly. _____

2. Music and dance (have) kept the Fine Arts Department solvent. _____

3. Either the clocks or the refrigerator (make) an annoying buzzing sound. _____

4. Elaine or one of her classmates (help) every afternoon at the pool. _____

5. Peaches and cream (be) my favorite dessert. _____

6. Every man and woman in this room (have) the right to express an opinion. _____

7. Either the characters or the plot (need) revising before your story can be published. _____

8. Track and field (be) one of the choices for your next physical education class. _____

9. Neither the bushes nor the tree (give) any shade during the afternoon. _____

10. After the prices change, each poster and price tag (have) to be corrected. _____

11. Both the paving bricks and the mortar (be) on sale this week. _____

12. Rock and roll (be) the subject of the display at the museum. _____

B. Correcting Errors in Agreement

For each sentence or clause with a compound subject, decide whether the subject and verb agree. If they do not, write the correct present tense verb. If they do, write ***Correct.***

1. Both a beginner's bicycle and a utility bike has level handlebars. _____

2. Drop handlebars and racing saddles are found on lightweight bikes. _____

3. Neither a unicycle nor a tandem bike is appropriate for everyday use. _____

4. Stability and large baskets makes tricycles appealing to some adults. _____

5. Each nut and bolt need to be examined before you buy a bicycle. _____

6. If either the spokes or the wheel seem defective, be careful. _____

7. Reflectors and a light is necessary if you ride your bike at night. _____

8. A generator or batteries provide power for the light. _____

9. Either a rack or a basket give you a way to carry things. _____

10. Some tools for repairs and a good lock completes your accessories. _____

CHAPTER 5

Lesson 3 | # Compound Subjects | *Application*

A. Combining Sentences Using Compound Subjects

Rewrite the following paragraph, combining sentences where possible by using compound subjects. Use *and, or, nor, either/or,* or *neither/nor* to join the parts of a subject. Keep the action in the tense of the two original sentences that are joined.

My mother does not like animals. My father also does not like animals. However, my little sister loves all animals, especially dogs. I feel the same about animals. So, a puppy is a pet we want our parents to buy for us. Alternatively, a kitten is something we want our parents to buy. Friends with pets admit they are a lot of work and responsibility. Every relative of ours with pets admits that fact. If we get a dog, my parents demand that my sister walk it every day. Or my parents demand that I walk it every day. Cats do not need walks. Kittens do not need walks. On the other hand, my parents dislike litter boxes in the house. I also do not want a litter box in the house. Baths are one of the responsibilities pet owners have. Another responsibility pet owners have is taking their pet to see the veterinarian. My sister does not let responsibilities scare her away from the joys of pet ownership, however. Nor do I let them scare me.

_____

_____

_____

_____

_____

_____

_____

_____

B. Using the Correct Verb with Compound Subjects

Write a sentence with each type of subject named.

1. (compound subject whose parts are joined by *and*) _____

_____

2. (compound subject whose parts are joined by *or* that takes a singular verb) _____

_____

3. (compound subject whose parts are joined by *or* that takes a plural verb) _____

_____

CHAPTER 5

Other Confusing Subjects

Lesson 4

Teaching

Collective nouns name groups of people or things. Examples include *council, flock,* and *family.* If a collective noun subject refers to the group as a unit, it takes a singular verb. If the noun refers to members of the group as individuals, it takes a plural verb.

> The orchestra **is** world-famous. (seen as one)
> On break, the orchestra **are** all over the building. (seen separately)

Phrases or clauses that serve as subjects of sentences always take singular verbs.

> Auditioning for the orchestra **is** not an easy experience.

Some nouns ending in *–s* appear to be plural but are singular in meaning and therefore take a singular verb. Examples include *measles* and *molasses.* Nouns ending in *–ics,* such as *mathematics* and *physics,* are almost always singular. A few such words—*ethics* and *acoustics* for example—can be singular or plural depending on the context.

> Acoustics **is** the study of sound.
> The acoustics in this hall **provide** an excellent setting for the orchestra.

Certain nouns ending in *–s,* such as *scissors, pants, shorts* and *glasses,* take plural verbs even though they name one thing.

Numerical amounts and titles of works of art, literature, or music are considered singular. Fractional numbers are singular when they refer to a singular noun and plural when they refer to a plural noun.

> *Pictures at an Exhibition* **is** on the program. Two-thirds of it **has** been played.

Using Verbs That Agree with Problem Subjects

In each sentence, underline the subject and the form of the verb that agrees with it. If the subject is a fractional number, underline twice the word it refers to.

1. Twenty minutes of exercise (is, are) recommended by many experts in the health field.

2. A pair of pheasants (was, were) sitting in the long grass.

3. "A penny saved is a penny earned" (is, are) a proverb by Benjamin Franklin.

4. (Is, Are) $50 a fair price for a ticket to a hockey game?

5. Whether we will be allowed to lift off before the other planes on the runway (has, have) not yet been decided.

6. Astrophysics (is, are) concerned with the physical qualities of heavenly bodies.

7. The realistic *Nighthawks* (was, were) painted by Edward Hopper in 1942.

8. Four-tenths of the voters (has, have) not voted today.

9. To find my lost contact lens (is, are) my top priority at the moment.

10. The jury (has, have) been allowed to go to their homes finally.

11. Aerobics (is, are) designed to improve one's cardiovascular system.

12. Well-sharpened scissors (cut, cuts) cleanly through the cloth.

13. One-fifth of the winter (is, are) behind us.

14. Cleaning these pots and pans (require, requires) real scrubbing.

Lesson 4

Other Confusing Subjects

More Practice

A. Using Verbs That Agree with Problem Subjects

In each sentence, underline the verb that agrees in number with the subject.

1. *Burmese Days* (describe, describes) life in the Far East before World War II.

2. The staff at Valley Lake Day Camp (hold, holds) one meeting each week.

3. Raking leaves into the streets (is, are) allowed through November.

4. For Debra, physics (is, are) a passion.

5. Carrying all those boxes into the garage (seem, seems) like a big job.

6. Two-thirds of the crackers (is, are) crushed.

7. The League of Women Voters (was, were) registering all eligible voters in town.

8. The news often (depress, depresses) us with reports of violent events.

9. Putting too many purchases on charge cards (is, are) a dangerous practice.

10. Ten minutes (seem, seems) like an eternity at times.

11. "Romeo, Romeo. Wherefore art thou Romeo?" (is, are) a line from *Romeo and Juliet* that is often misunderstood.

12. To bring in a consultant at this stage of the proceedings (strike, strikes) me as a waste of money.

B. Writing Sentences

Complete each of these sentences by adding a present-tense verb as described in the parentheses. Add any other needed words.

EXAMPLE (singular verb)   Three-tenths *of the wall is already painted.*

1. (singular verb)   Our baseball team _____

_____

2. (plural verb)   Our baseball team _____

_____

3. (plural verb)   Four-fifths _____

_____

4. (singular verb)   Four-fifths _____

_____

5. (singular verb)   The dance committee _____

_____

6. (plural verb)   The dance committee _____

_____

Lesson 4 · Other Confusing Subjects   *Application*

A. Proofreading for Subject-Verb Agreement

Proofread this paragraph for errors in subject-verb agreement. Draw a line through each incorrect verb. Then draw this proofreading symbol ⌄ next to the word and write the correction above the error.

      The soccer club in town form a travel team every year. Advertising for the team are an easy task. Eighteen students from the high school plays for the travel team. A committee from the club chooses which students will play. News of the committee's choices travel quickly around the school. The team practices are long and grueling. Three miles are the usual distance of the practice runs. The uniform shorts is blue, while the uniform shirt is white. The crowd that watches the games are always very enthusiastic. This encourages the team because traveling 50 miles or more to get to games are not unusual. Simple mathematics tell us that an average of 150 people attend the weekly games.

B. Using Confusing Subjects Correctly in Writing

Write a short sports article about a sport you like, as if reporting on an event. In the article use each of the phrases below as subjects of sentences, as indicated. In addition, use at least one noun clause as a subject.

    The coaching staff (used with singular verb)   The news
    The coaching staff (used with plural verb)   10,000 fans

_____

_____

_____

_____

_____

_____

_____

_____

_____

_____

_____

_____

CHAPTER 5

Lesson 5 # Special Agreement Problems *Teaching*

The form of some sentences can make identifying their subjects difficult.

In an **inverted statement** and many **questions,** the subject follows the verb or part of the verb phrase. Rearrange the words in standard order to find the subject, and then choose the correct verb.

Is the <u>gym</u> open? The <u>gym</u> **is** open.

Down **came** the <u>balls</u> from the top shelf. The <u>balls</u> **came** down from the top shelf.

An **imperative sentence** may not state the subject; it is almost always *you.*

(<u>You</u>) **Show** your ID and pass at the front desk.

In most sentences beginning with *here* or *there,* the subject usually follows the verb.

There **are** <u>lockers</u> that you can rent by the day or week.

In a sentence with a **predicate nominative,** the verb must agree with the subject, not the predicate nominative.

Aerobic <u>exercises</u> **are** one way to build stamina. One <u>way</u> to build stamina **is** aerobic exercises.

When a relative pronoun—*who, which,* or *that*—is the subject of an adjective clause, its number is determined by its antecedent.

The lifeguards <u>who</u> **work** weekends are friendly. (refers to *lifeguards,* plural)

The lifeguard <u>who</u> **works** tonight is new. (refers to *lifeguard,* singular)

Solving Agreement Problems

In each sentence, underline the subject (if it is stated). Then underline the correct verb.

1. There (is, are) no excuses for avoiding daily exercise.
2. Exercises (is, are) a way of improving mood as well as muscle.
3. (Has, Have) the schedule for the pool changed lately?
4. Here at the recreation center (is, are) many valuable programs.
5. Behind the building (is, are) a running track for summer use.
6. Inside (is, are) treadmills, rowing machines, and stationary bikes.
7. The parents who (bring, brings) their children for classes often exercise, too.
8. When (do, does) the swimming classes for beginners start?
9. One sign of an unhealthy body (is, are) puny muscles.
10. In the green cabinet across the hall (is, are) the volleyballs.
11. The piece of equipment that (is, are) the busiest is the new treadmill.
12. The colorful plastic lines (is, are) the separation between the two parts of the pool.
13. There (is, are) stretching, weight-lifting, and aerobics classes on the weekend.
14. On the bulletin board (is, are) the sign-up sheet.
15. Parking spaces for the handicapped (is, are) a clear indication that the center is used by all groups in the community.
16. Why (is, are) the pool closing early on Sunday?
17. The rec center's front door, which (is, are) always open, is opposite the post office.
18. Before leaving, (remember, remembers) to sign out.

Lesson 5

Special Agreement Problems

More Practice

A. Solving Agreement Problems

In each sentence, find and underline the subject if it is stated. Then write the present tense form of the verb that agrees with the subject.

1. (Do) the Bloomsbury Group include Virginia Woolf?

2. Ralph is the guide who (lead) the Saturday morning walks.

3. Here (be) a picture of two of them.

4. Are these the vases that (belong) to Mrs. Peabody?

5. Novels (be) the Victorians' legacy.

6. Here (be) the Byron poems I told you about.

7. This is a movie for people who (need) a pick-me-up.

8. Here (come) some of our noisiest relatives!

9. Those old travel guides (be) still an authoritative source.

10. What he cared about (be) words.

11. Ask the guard who (be) standing at the front door when the store will open.

12. Books (be) the obsession of the bibliophile.

13. We opened every box that (have) your name on it, but we couldn't find the sweaters you packed.

14. There but for fortune (go) we.

B. Making Subjects and Verbs Agree

Complete each quotation with the correct form of the verb *be*.

1. There _____ nothing in this world constant, but inconstancy.
   Jonathan Swift

2. Art for Art's sake _____ an empty phrase.
   George Sand

3. Reviewers _____ usually people who would have been poets, historians, biographers, etc., if they could.
   Samuel Taylor Coleridge

4. Language _____ the archives of history.
   Ralph Waldo Emerson

5. Every mile _____ two in winter.
   George Herbert

CHAPTER 5

Special Agreement Problems   *Application*

A. Using Sentence Variety and Agreement

All these items have errors in subject-verb agreement. Before rewriting each sentence or pair of sentences with correct agreement, make the change indicated in parentheses.

EXAMPLE Two baby birds rests under their mother's wings. (Change subject-verb order.)

Under their mother's wings rest two baby birds.

1. Here is Nancy's treasure. Here is dozens of two-inch stuffed dolls. (Combine the sentences using a predicate nominative.)

_____

2. A large park full of beautiful trees are across the street. (Change subject-verb order.)

_____

3. The team is playing against us on Saturday. The team are leading the league. (Combine sentences using a subordinate clause.)

_____

4. The bus are coming. (Use *Here* to begin the sentence.)

_____

5. The others on your team are wearing their shorts in this cold weather. (Change the statement into a question.)

_____

B. Writing with Sentence Variety and Subject-Verb Agreement

Choose one of the topics below and write a paragraph of at least seven sentences, including these: 1) a sentence, either a statement or question, with inverted order of subject and verb; 2) a sentence beginning with *here* or *there*; 3) a sentence with a predicate nominative. Be sure to use correct subject-verb agreement in every sentence.

My worst nightmare   My favorite time of day

A friend who always makes me laugh   What I do to relax

_____

_____

_____

_____

_____

_____

CHAPTER 5

Nominative and Objective Cases

Teaching

Personal pronouns change form depending on how they function in a sentence. The form of a pronoun is called its **case**. The cases are nominative, objective, and possessive.

		Nominative	Objective	Possessive
Singular	**First Person**	I	me	my, mine
	Second Person	you	you	your, yours
	Third Person	he, she, it	him, her, it	his, her, hers, its
Plural	**First Person**	we	us	our, ours
	Second Person	you	you	your, yours
	Third Person	they	them	their, theirs

The **nominative form** of a personal pronoun is used when the pronoun functions as a subject, as part of a compound subject, or as a predicate nominative. A pronoun used as a predicate nominative is called a **predicate pronoun**. It takes the nominative case.

SUBJECT	<u>She</u> is my mother's niece.
PART OF COMPOUND SUBJECT	<u>She</u> and <u>I</u> are cousins.
PREDICATE PRONOUN	The cousin I most resemble is <u>she</u>.

The **objective form** of a personal pronoun is used when the pronoun functions as a direct object, indirect object, or object of a preposition. Use it also when the pronoun is part of a compound object, or when it's used with an infinitive. An **infinitive** is the base form of a verb preceded by the word *to —to visit, to jog, to play.*

DIRECT OBJECT	You can see <u>her</u> in these old family portraits.
INDIRECT OBJECT	My aunt sent <u>me</u> invitations to her wedding.
OBJECT OF PREPOSITION	A distant cousin has been searching for <u>us</u>.
PART OF COMPOUND OBJECT	My aunt reserved rooms for <u>them</u> and <u>us</u>.
INFINITIVE	Julie and Courtney went to visit <u>him</u>.

To decide which case to use in a compound construction, consider each part separately.

A. Identifying the Case of a Pronoun

Identify the case of each boldfaced personal pronoun in the following sentences. On the line write **N** for nominative or **O** for objective.

1. My uncle, my mother's brother, is an attorney, but **he** really only wants to paint. _____

2. He painted a portrait of my mother and gave it to **her** as a wedding present. _____

3. My mother painted, too, but **she** said he was the talented one. _____

4. She said their mother had wanted **them** both to go to art school. _____

5. My mother said, "I wish **we** both had listened to her." _____

B. Using the Correct Case of Personal Pronouns

Underline the correct pronoun to complete each sentence.

1. It was (he, him) who made the posters for our election campaign.

2. When will Burt and (I, me) get our turn to participate in that program?

3. The extreme wind-chill factor left Teresa and (I, me) shivering.

Lesson 1

Nominative and Objective Cases

More Practice

A. Using the Correct Case of Personal Pronouns

In each sentence, underline the correct pronoun form.

1. My grandfather was a carpenter; (he, him) made beautiful cabinets.
2. My grandmother baked a pie for (we, us) every Sunday.
3. (Her, She) and I used to go shopping together.
4. She taught (me, I) how to cook and sew.
5. Baking was harder, and I never could do it as well as (her, she).
6. Women of the family have to help each other out, (she, her) said.
7. My grandfather and (she, her) didn't always get along.
8. (They, Them) were my grandparents on my father's side.
9. My mother's parents lived in Texas, so we didn't see (them, they) very often.
10. They sent me a chess set, and I still have (it, them).
11. When I was 13, I flew to Texas to visit (them, they).
12. My Texas grandmother and (me, I) went shopping in Austin.

B. Choosing Personal Pronouns

In the following sentences, fill in the blanks with the appropriate personal pronouns. Vary the person and number of the pronouns, and do not use the pronoun *you*.

1. The mail carrier brought _____ the current edition of the magazine.

2. Corinne and _____ discussed the plays of Arthur Miller.

3. The swimming coach sent Evan and _____ to a special backstroke coach.

4. Despite early difficulties, _____ and the rest of the cast got along well.

5. I am certain that I gave _____ the tickets.

6. It must have been _____ who sang a Verdi opera.

7. Be sure to leave the extra copies of the flyer for _____ and _____.

8. If you need a ride home, call Frank's dad or _____.

9. After graduation, my parents gave my twin and _____ a trip to Washington.

10. Are Michelle and _____ responsible for closing the theater?

CHAPTER 6

Name _____ Date _____

Nominative and Objective Cases

Application

A. Proofreading

Proofread the following story to make sure that the correct cases of pronouns have been used. When you find a pronoun used incorrectly, cross it out. Then insert this proofreading symbol ⁁ and write the correct pronoun above it.

     If you and me had the same mother and father, then we would be sister

and brother. If we had only one parent in common, however, our relationship

would be different. Him and her, for example, both have the same father, but

not the same mother. George and her are half brother and half sister. Did I tell

you about Jackie and him, who are stepsister and stepbrother? We know she

and him from school. Jackie and him don't have either parent in common.

Jackie's father and Bill's mother are married to each other, but that marriage

didn't make him Bill's father or her Jackie's mother.

B. Using Personal Pronouns in Writing

Write a paragraph about your own (or a friend's) family, describing the relationships among the various members. Be sure to use personal pronouns correctly.

_____

_____

_____

_____

_____

_____

_____

_____

_____

_____

_____

_____

_____

_____

Lesson 2 Possessive Case

Personal pronouns that show ownership or relationship are in the **possessive case**. The possessive pronouns *mine, ours, yours, his, hers, its*, and *theirs* can be used in place of a noun. They can function as subjects, predicate nominatives, or objects.

> Different forms of government have been tried. <u>Ours</u> is a democracy.

The possessive pronouns *my, your, his, her, its*, and *their* can be used to modify nouns or gerunds. The pronoun precedes the noun or gerund it modifies. Do not use a possessive pronoun with a participle.

> <u>Their</u> relying on the common people rather than on nobility for leadership determined the form of our government. (*relying* used as gerund)

> The nobility laughed at <u>them</u>, relying on commoners. (*relying* used as participle)

Don't confuse these possessive pronouns with the contractions that they sound like: their/they're (they are), its/it's (it is), your/you're (you are).

A. Identifying Possessive Pronouns

Underline all the possessive pronouns in each sentence.

1. The dictator's emotional appeal was responsible for his gaining absolute power.

2. He appealed to the poor by telling them he would eradicate their misery by passing laws against the rich and redistributing their wealth.

3. His winning over the middle class was due to a promise to give them fewer taxes.

4. He told the rich that their fear of his seizing their wealth was groundless.

5. Listening to our emotions rather than to our intellects can allow a dictator to impose his will on our country.

B. Using Personal Pronouns Correctly

In each sentence, underline the correct pronoun form.

1. The French overthrew (theirs, their) kings.

2. Yet they accepted Napoleon as (their, they're) emperor.

3. In 1776, the United States was unique because of (us, our) rejecting kingship.

4. More than 200 years later, the idea of a monarchy retains (it's, its) popularity in parts of the world.

5. Doris and (me, I) argued about what political system was best.

6. I said, "(You're, Your) opinion of what's best for a country must be based on the history and traditions of that country."

7. She said, "I don't even understand (mine, my) own country's history and traditions."

8. I said, "Some kings were very kind and beneficial to (their, they're) people."

9. "I suppose it's the same with (our, ours) elected officials," she said.

10. (She, Her) saying that made me think more about our own system.

11. "(Your, You're) right," I said. "We have good and bad officials, too."

12. "But our system is the best for (we, us)," she said, and (I, me) agreed.

Lesson 2 **Possessive Case**   *More Practice*

A. Using Personal Pronouns Correctly

In each sentence, underline the correct pronoun form.

1. Napoleon marched (his, him) troops into Russia.

2. (His, Him) not planning how he would feed the army during the winter of 1812 resulted in its destruction.

3. My father gave my brother and (me, my) a copy of the novel *War and Peace*.

4. In his novel, Leo Tolstoy describes Napoleon's campaign and (its, it's) failure.

5. At the same time, the United States was fighting (its, it's) own War of 1812.

6. Our war with the British concerned the boundary line between our territory and (they're, theirs) in North America.

7. It also was about (their, them) removing American sailors from American ships to serve on British ships.

8. We need writers to tell (our, ours) history as magnificently as Tolstoy told Russia's.

9. You could say that (he, his) made history as much as Napoleon and the Tsar did.

10. Maybe the nation as a whole—not the rulers—makes (their, its) own history.

B. Using Pronouns to Emphasize Actions and Actors

Write a sentence using each of the given phrases. Do not use the same verb in more than one sentence.

EXAMPLES   me writing the letter
           My cat watched me writing the letter.
           my writing the letter
           My writing the letter was unusual; usually I telephone.

1. his buying a car _____

   _____

2. him singing along _____

   _____

3. her spilling the drink _____

   _____

4. us going to our seats _____

   _____

5. your finding the wallet _____

   _____

Possessive Case

Lesson 2

Application

A. Proofreading for Pronoun Errors

Proofread the following essay. When you find a possessive pronoun used incorrectly, cross it out. Insert this proofreading symbol ‸ and write the correct pronoun above it.

France is now a republic. It elects it's leaders. But France was a monarchy

from the Middle Ages to the time of the French Revolution, which occurred

just after ours Revolution and was inspired by it's success. A monarchy is a

state ruled by kings. In America, ours idea of royalty is that its a primitive and

inferior form of government. But consider the history of the French people.

During the Middle Ages, they're form of government was feudal, with many

little states or realms. Them having this system hindered trade and commerce

and led to much fighting among there realms. In 987 the nobles chose Hugh

Capet as their king. Him starting the Capetian dynasty eventually resulted in a

strong central government under his descendants. In times of peace, trade

and commerce could grow as never before.

B. Using Pronoun Cases Correctly in Writing

Write a paragraph relating facts about a ruler in a country, either past or present, that is not or was not a democracy at the time of that ruler. For example, the ruler could be a king, queen, emperor, or dictator. Use the correct cases of personal pronouns in your sentences. Be sure to use at least four pronouns in the possessive case. In addition, use each of these phrases appropriately:

them (or him, her, it) having   their (or his, her, its) having

_____

_____

_____

_____

_____

_____

_____

_____

CHAPTER 6

Lesson 3

Who and *Whom*

Teaching

The case of the pronoun **who** is determined by the pronoun's function in the sentence.

Nominative	who, whoever
Objective	whom, whomever
Possessive	whose, whosever

Who and *whom* can be used to ask questions and to introduce subordinate clauses. *Whose* and *whosever* can be used to show ownership or relationship.

In a question, *who* is used as subject or predicate pronoun. The objective pronoun *whom* is used as a direct or indirect object of a verb or as object of a preposition.

SUBJECT   Who is being considered for the chemistry award?
DIRECT OBJECT   Whom did the awards jury interview so far?
OBJECT OF PREPOSITION   To whom was the award given last year?

When deciding whether to use *who* or *whom* in a subordinate clause, consider only how the pronoun functions in the clause. If it is the subject, use *who*. If the pronoun is an object in the subordinate clause, use *whom*.

SUBJECT OF CLAUSE   Anyone who nominates a candidate completes a form.
OBJECT IN CLAUSE   Those whom the jury interviews go on to the next stage.

Using *Who* and *Whom* Correctly

In each sentence, underline the correct pronoun form. If the pronoun choice is in a subordinate clause, first draw brackets [ ] before and after the clause. Decide how the pronoun functions in the clause. Then mark the right choice.

Give your application to [(whoever, whomever) is at the desk].

1. Antoine Lavoisier, (who, whom) was executed during the French Revolution, was one of the founders of modern chemistry.

2. (Who, Whom) will follow in the footsteps of the great men and women of science?

3. Alchemists, (who, whom) were predecessors of true chemists, tried to turn lead into gold.

4. They got their ideas from (whoever, whomever) they found promising.

5. (Who, Whom) among the ancient Greeks could be considered a chemist?

6. From (who, whom) did we get the notion of atoms?

7. Chinese chemists (whose, whosever) names we don't know invented gunpowder.

8. (Who, Whom) did Lavoisier influence?

9. The professor asked (who, whom) could define the term *stoichiometry*.

10. She offered an extra 5 points to (whomever, whoever) explained the term.

11. The student (who, whom) I sat behind had the answer.

12. (Who, Whom) did Aristotle get his ideas from?

13. We all know (who, whom) discovered radioactivity.

14. But (who, whom) first used it to produce x-rays?

15. (Whoever, Whomever) wants to study chemistry should take some math.

Lesson 3

Who and *Whom*

More Practice

A. Identifying the Functions of *Who* and *Whom*

In the following sentences, determine the function of *who/whoever* or *whom/whomever*. If a sentence uses *who* or *whoever*, underline once the verb of which it is the subject. If a sentence uses *whom* or *whomever*, underline twice the verb or preposition of which it is an object.

> **EXAMPLES**   Scientists **who** <u>read</u> Shakespeare are well-rounded.
>
> That student will disagree with **whomever** he <u>dislikes</u>.

1. To **whom** was the Nobel Prize for chemistry awarded in 1932?

2. **Whoever** founded the Nobel Prize?

3. Do the judges give the award to **whomever** they like?

4. No, they give it to **whoever** they believe did the most important work.

5. Alfred Nobel, for **whom** the prizes are named, made his fortune with explosives.

6. He was a Swedish chemist **who** invented dynamite with the hope of making work conditions safer for miners and others whose work required handling explosives.

7. Noble wanted to assure that **whoever** did valuable work in physics, chemistry, physiology and medicine, literature, and humanitarian fields received recognition.

8. Linus Pauling, **who** won two Nobel Prizes, examined chemical bonds.

9. **Who** won the award for work on quantum theory?

10. That was Niels Bohr, **whom** the judges awarded the prize for physics in 1922.

B. Using Forms of *Who* Correctly

In each sentence, underline the correct pronoun form.

1. (Whoever, Whomever) leaves the room last should turn off the lights.

2. Do you know (who, whom, whose) invented the zipper?

3. The architect (who, whom, whose) design wins will get a profitable contract.

4. Shakespeare is a playwright about (who, whom, whose) I would like to know more.

5. Our so-called watchdog wants (whoever, whomever) walks into the yard to pet her.

6. Did Marie find out (who, whom) Jerry is giving the party for?

7. (Who, Whom) did they say won the last race?

8. Offer the tickets to (whoever, whomever, whosever) you meet in the lobby.

9. (Whoever, Whomever, Whosever) score is highest wins the game.

10. Please ask (who, whom) the speaker is.

11. The painters (who, whom) Dad hired are late.

12. Nobody can remember for (who, whom) we saved this moldy sandwich.

13. Only those students (who, whom, whose) last names begin with *M* should stand.

14. Tell (whoever, whomever) was scheduled to work tonight about the power outage.

15. The bus driver invited the students (who, whom) he picks up regularly to a picnic.

CHAPTER 6

Who and *Whom*

Application

A. Proofreading for *Who* and *Whom*

Proofread the following paragraph. Decide whether each numbered use of form a of *who* is correct. If the wrong form of the pronoun is used, write the correct form on the line below. If the correct form is used, write **Correct.**

Madame Marie Curie, **(1)** whom was awarded two Nobel Prizes, was a martyr to modern chemistry. Her first Nobel Prize, in 1903, for pioneer work on radioactivity, was shared two men—her husband, Pierre Curie, **(2)** whom she had married in 1895, and Henri Becquerel, **(3)** whom discovered radioactivity. The second, in 1911, was for her discovery of the radioactive elements radium and polonium. Her work with these materials led to her contracting leukemia, a form of cancer, which killed her. But **(4)** whom at the time knew these materials were dangerous? **(5)** Whoever works with such materials today does so from behind heavy shielding or in special protective clothing. We, **(6)** whom recognize the dangers of these materials, and **(7)** whom Madame Curie's work with them benefits, use radium as a basic material in chemotherapy, to cure cancer.

Madame Curie was also the mother of Irene Joliot-Curie, **(8)** whom was awarded the Nobel Prize in chemistry in 1935. Joliot-Curie also shared the prize with her husband, Frederic Joliot-Curie, **(9)** who she had married in 1926.

1. _____   4. _____   7. _____

2. _____   5. _____   8. _____

3. _____   6. _____   9. _____

B. Using *Who, Whom,* and *Whose* in Writing

Rewrite each sentence or pair of sentences below as a single sentence that uses a subordinate clause introduced by or containing *who, whom,* or *whose.* Use the pronoun given in parentheses in your new sentence.

EXAMPLE I will ask that man. He is selling newspapers. (who)
I will ask the man who is selling newspapers.

1. The teacher reprimanded the student. His assignment was late. (whose)

_____

2. This is the phone number of the young lady. You wanted to ask her out. (whom)

_____

3. Some students studied hard. They got good grades. (whoever)

_____

4. My neighbor is an excellent gardener. Every year he gives me tomatoes. (who)

_____

5. He interviewed all of the people he had met at the concert. (whomever)

_____

④ Pronoun-Antecedent Agreement   *Teaching*

A pronoun must agree with its antecedent in number, gender, and person. An **antecedent** is the noun or pronoun that a pronoun refers to or replaces.

If the antecedent is singular, use a singular pronoun. If it is plural, use a plural pronoun. Nouns or pronouns joined by *and* are treated as a plural antecedent. If parts of the antecedent are joined by *or* or *nor*, the pronoun agrees with the part nearest to it.

> Both the <u>officers and the captain</u> have <u>their</u> names on the ship's newsletter.
> Either the officers or the <u>captain</u> has <u>his</u> quarters at the end of this hall.

With Indefinite Pronouns Use a singular personal pronoun to refer to a singular **indefinite pronoun,** and a plural personal pronoun to refer to a plural indefinite pronoun.

> <u>Each</u> of the ships has its own dock. <u>Many</u> of the ships are loading <u>their</u> supplies.

Indefinite Pronouns

Always Singular					Always Plural	Singular or Plural	
another	each	everything	no one	someone	both	all	most
anybody	either	much	nothing	something	few	any	none
anyone	everybody	neither	one		many	more	some
anything	everyone	nobody	somebody		several		

If the indefinite pronoun antecedent can be singular or plural, use the meaning of the sentence to determine the number of the indefinite personal pronoun.

> <u>Most</u> of the entertainment delighted <u>its</u> audience. (singular)
> <u>Most</u> of the entertainers were on <u>their</u> first cruise. (plural)

Gender and Person If the antecedent of a singular pronoun could be either feminine or masculine, use the phrase *his or her*. The indefinite pronouns *one, everyone*, and *everybody* are in the third person, so pronouns referring to them must be third person also.

Making Pronouns and Their Antecedents Agree

In each sentence, underline the correct pronoun and its antecedent.

> <u>All</u> of the <u>lifeboats</u> have had (its, <u>their</u>) supplies renewed.

1. The captain is French, but (their, his) wife is Italian.
2. They spent (their, his) honeymoon on a cruise ship.
3. The captain and the first mate are on (their, his) first voyage together.
4. Neither the petty officers nor the captain wants (his, their) orders questioned.
5. Many buy (their, his) souvenirs at the harbor store.
6. Some of the food on the buffet was so beautiful that we took (its, their) picture.

CHAPTER 6

Pronoun-Antecedent Agreement

More Practice

A. Making Pronouns and Antecedents Agree

Underline the pronoun in parentheses that correctly completes each sentence.
Also underline the antecedent(s) of the pronoun.

1. Each of the boys enjoyed (his, their) week at the baseball training camp.
2. Some of the swimathon participants arrived with (his or her, their) sponsors.
3. Either Janet or Marjorie left (her, their) calculus book on the windowsill.
4. The chorus honored (its, their) director at a banquet this spring,
5. Most of the antique furniture still had (its, their) original upholstery.
6. Everyone is invited to test (your, his or her, their) ability to climb the wall.
7. The City Council presented (its, their) varying opinions to the media.
8. Either the president or members of Congress will have (his, their) pictures taken.
9. Several of the delegates tried to resolve (its, his or her, their) conflicting views.
10. Some of the wallpaper in those rooms shows (its, their) age.

B. Using Pronouns Correctly

In each sentence below, decide whether the pronouns agree with their antecedents.
If the sentence is correct, write **Correct** on the line. If it contains a pronoun that does
not agree with its antecedent, rewrite the sentence correctly on the line.

1. Some of the crew on the cruise ship traveled far from its homelands.

   _____

2. One of the officers has had their license for only a week.

   _____

3. In my view, all of the ship lived up to their publicity.

   _____

4. A few of the passengers complained about the size of their rooms.

   _____

5. One of the women passengers stayed in their room for the first two days.

   _____

6. The captain and the officers took his meals with the passengers.

   _____

7. Everybody had their chance to sit at the captain's table.

   _____

8. Either the captain or the first mate was always at their post on the bridge.

   _____

Pronoun-Antecedent Agreement

Lesson 4

Application

A. Making Pronouns and Antecedents Agree in Writing

Read the following paragraph. Look especially for errors in agreement between pronouns and their antecedents. On the lines below, write the numbers of the sentences with agreement errors. Then write each of those sentences correctly.

(1) My parents went on a cruise for his or her thirtieth anniversary. (2) Neither one had ever been away from their family for a week. (3) My mother tried to get her mother to go along, but she wouldn't. (4) The whole family agreed that it was good for them to get away on your own. (5) Everyone on the ship got to know my parents and gave them their address. (6) My father wanted to swim in the pool, but he had forgotten his swimming trunks. (7) They won the shuffleboard tournament for their age group. (8) The captain and my father had his picture taken shaking hands. (9) My parents liked the captain and crew for its friendliness. (10) They said they'd like to go again, but this time with their family.

_____

_____

_____

_____

_____

_____

_____

_____

B. Writing with Pronouns

Have you ever been on a vessel on water or imagined going on such a voyage? Was it a canoe on a slow-moving river, a cruise ship on an ocean, or something in between? Write a description of a voyage you have taken or imagined, including mention of the crew (if only yourself), fellow passengers (if any), and the reason for your trip. Be sure to include at least five personal pronouns with clear antecedents.

_____

_____

_____

_____

_____

_____

_____

CHAPTER 6

Other Pronoun Problems

Teaching

Lesson 5

A pronoun may be used with an appositive, in an appositive, or in a comparison. An **appositive** is a noun or pronoun that follows another noun or pronoun and identifies or renames it. The pronoun *we* or *us* may be followed by an appositive. To determine whether to use *we* or *us*, drop the appositive from the sentence, and determine whether the pronoun is a subject or an object.

> We dining critics have high standards.   (We have high standards.)
> This restaurant pleased us critics.   (The restaurant pleased us.)

A pronoun used in an appositive is in the same case it would take if the noun were missing.

> The chefs, Abel and she, planned the menu. (*She* acts as a subject of *planned*.)
> We congratulated the chefs, Abel and her. (*Her* acts as an object of *congratulated*.)

Pronouns in Comparisons   You can make a comparison using *than* or *as* to begin a clause. If you omit the final words of the clause, it is said to be **elliptical**. To determine the correct pronoun to use in an elliptical clause, mentally fill in the unstated words.

> Alain appreciates fine food more than I.   (more than I appreciate fine food)
> Alain appreciates fine food more than me. (more than Alain appreciates me)

Reflexive and Intensive Pronouns   A pronoun ending in *–self* or *–selves* may be used reflexively; that is, it refers to a preceding noun or pronoun. The same pronoun used intensively simply adds emphasis. It is incorrect to use a reflexive pronoun or an intensive pronoun without an antecedent.

> I myself prepared the soufflé.   (used as intensive pronoun)
> I blamed myself for the ruined soufflé. (used as reflexive pronoun)

A. Choosing the Correct Pronoun

In each sentence, underline the correct pronoun form.

1. (Us, We) chefs can sometimes seem arrogant and opinionated.
2. Maurice uses different techniques than (I, me).
3. They interviewed two chefs, Louise and (he, him), for the opening.
4. They would have interviewed (myself, me), too, but I wasn't interested.
5. You usually eat more than (me, I).
6. The last couple to arrive, Fred and (her, she), were late for the first course.
7. Next time, they (theirselves, themselves) can prepare their own dinner.
8. Tomorrow they will interview (we, us) applicants for the busboy opening.

B. Using Reflexive and Intensive Pronouns Correctly

In each set, underline the correct sentence.

1. If you have prepared this dish yourself, give me some pointers. / If yourself have prepared this dish, give me some pointers.
2. Rita limited herself to 300 calories. / Rita limited Rita to 300 calories.
3. Don't let myself influence your choice. / Don't let me influence your choice
4. Himself the chef prefers hot dogs. / The chef himself prefers hot dogs.

Lesson 5 # Other Pronoun Problems   *More Practice*

A. Choosing the Correct Pronoun

In each sentence, underline the correct pronoun form.

1. Elena is as good a hockey player as (he, him).
2. The volunteers, you and (they, them), will handle the phones tonight.
3. The matter is strictly between (we, us) bikers and them.
4. (Myself, I myself) never noticed how late it was.
5. Tomorrow (we, us) shoppers will hurry to the sales.
6. Coach Leone played Chris more than (I, me).
7. The clerk told the shoppers, the Hills and (we, us), that the store was closing.
8. (We, Us) writers sometimes work late to meet our deadlines.
9. Benjamin told (he, himself) to pay attention to the alarm clock in the morning.
10. Mom is better at building bookcases than (she, her).
11. Heavy traffic made the bus riders, Gregory and (she, her), late for school again.
12. The manager asked (we, us) new workers to stay late.
13. Both singers, Walter and (her, she), plan to try out for the next musical.
14. The loud radio in that car is deafening both the driver and (we, us) pedestrians on the same street.
15. Probably, more people have heard him than (we, us).

B. Using Pronouns Correctly

Write an appropriate pronoun on the line in each sentence. Do not use the pronoun *you* or any possessive pronoun.

1. The waiter gave us and _____ a laugh with his fake French accent.

2. Smart diners let _____ waiters guide them in choosing their menus.

3. _____ Europeans are less dependent on fast-food restaurants than Americans.

4. Pierre knows almost as much about this matter as _____.

5. Vondra _____ was curious about what was in the ratatouille.

6. _____ and Helena, the new students, ask many questions.

7. He prepares quiche almost as well as _____.

8. I taught _____ how to make mousse.

9. _____ connoisseurs should write a book.

10. Let's ask the waiters, Tom and _____.

CHAPTER 6

Lesson
5
Other Pronoun Problems

Application

A. Writing Elliptical Sentences Using Pronouns

Write an elliptical sentence with the same meaning as each of the following
sentences. Replace the boldfaced noun with a pronoun. Use the correct pronoun to
communicate your meaning.

> **EXAMPLE** Is Boris a better writer than **Natasha** is?
> *Is Boris a better writer than she?*

1. The artist who drew that portrait is more skillful than **Derek** is.

_____

2. The children phoned their online server more than **Grandma** phoned her server

_____

3. Roberto painted more props for the play than **Victor** painted.

_____

4. The children phoned their online server more than they phoned **Grandma**.

_____

5. Do you think that Gina works faster than **Mario** works?

_____

B. Proofreading for Correct Pronoun Usage

Proofread the following paragraph. When you find a pronoun used incorrectly, cross it
out. Then insert this proofreading symbol ⌃ and write the correct pronoun above it.

Us travelers to Paris love to eat in fine restaurants. In fact, nobody likes a

good sit-down dinner more than me. Still, travelers on a budget—Helen and

Mary and me, for example—sometimes have to save money by buying food in

a grocery store and eating it as we stroll and gawk. Helen and Mary don't like

to do this as much as me, but they theirselves said when we started out that

we shouldn't spend more than $1,000 apiece this trip. Mary's spending habits

are the worst. She said her and Helen, two of the pokiest walkers you ever

met, needed a balanced diet every day to keep up her strength for so much

sightseeing. Then she's always asking me—their personal accountant, it

seems—how much we've spent so far. Next time, I'm going to tell Mary to go

to her fancy restaurants by themselves. I'm not going to play budget police to

tourists who can't keep tabs on her own spending—Helen and she.

CHAPTER 6

Pronoun-Reference Problems

Lesson 6

Teaching

A pronoun should always refer clearly to a specific, stated antecedent.

General reference Readers may be confused when a pronoun refers to a general idea rather than to a specific noun. Correct the problem by rewriting the sentence(s) to make the antecedent clear or by replacing the pronoun with a noun or gerund.

> **AWKWARD** Leonardo Da Vinci's inventions were related to his art, which is not surprising.
>
> **REVISED** That Leonardo Da Vinci's inventions were related to his art is not surprising.

Indefinite reference Using a pronoun without any antecedent at all results in indefinite reference. Avoid using *it*, *you*, and *they* if they do not refer to a specific person or thing.

> **AWKWARD** In Leonardo's notebooks, you get drawings of his inventions.
>
> **REVISED** Leonardo's notebooks feature drawings of his inventions.

Ambiguous reference An ambiguous reference occurs when more than one possible antecedent exists for a pronoun. Indicate clearly what each pronoun refers to.

> **AWKWARD** Leonardo and Michelangelo were contemporaries; he was a painter, sculptor, architect, and poet.
>
> **REVISED** Leonardo and Michelangelo were contemporaries; Michelangelo was a painter, sculptor, architect, and poet.

Identifying Clear Pronoun References

In each pair of sentences below, one sentence has an indefinite, general, or ambiguous pronoun reference. The other is correct. Underline the one that is correct.

1. Isaac Newton and Gottfried Wilhelm von Leibniz invented calculus independently and at the same time; he was a scientist, philosopher, and diplomat.

   Isaac Newton and Gottfried Wilhelm von Leibniz invented calculus independently and at the same time; Leibniz was a scientist, philosopher, and diplomat.

2. Newton wrote on mathematics and optics, which was a great achievement.

   Newton's writing on mathematics and optics was a great achievement.

3. His *Principia Mathematica* includes a range of topics from gravitation to tides.

   In his *Principia Mathematica*, you get everything from gravitation to tides.

4. In the law of universal gravitation, it describes everything from apples falling from trees to the mutual attraction of stars and planets.

   The law of universal gravitation describes everything from apples falling from trees to the mutual attraction of stars and planets.

5. Newton probably never met Leibniz; he lived in Germany.

   Newton probably never met Leibniz, who lived in Germany.

6. Leibniz said the basic element of the universe is the monad, but that's simplistic.

   Leibniz said the basic constituent element of the universe is the monad, but the notion of the monad is simplistic.

7. Newton also worked in alchemy and astronomy, which contributed to what was called natural philosophy in his day.

   Newton's work in alchemy and astronomy contributed to what was called natural philosophy in his day.

CHAPTER 6

Pronoun-Reference Problems

More Practice

Avoiding Indefinite, General, and Ambiguous References

Rewrite the following sentences to correct indefinite, general, and ambiguous pronoun references. More than one interpretation may be possible. Add any words that are needed to make the meaning clear.

1. Thomas Edison, who invented the light bulb, didn't see the usefulness of electricity for power, which is hard to understand.

   _____

2. He and his assistants also invented things like the phonograph and moving pictures, and modern life would have been very different without them.

   _____

3. Among inventors, you have what could be called pure scientists and applied scientists.

   _____

4. Edison was clearly in the applied scientist category, where they develop scientific ideas into practical items.

   _____

5. In the pure scientist category, you have inventions that they come up with in the course of research, not by inventing to fill a need.

   _____

6. One "pure scientist" inventor was William Roentgen, who discovered the x-ray that resulted in the first x-ray photographs.

   _____

7. In between, you have people like Nikola Tesla, who worked with George Westinghouse; he once worked for Edison.

   _____

8. Tesla helped Westinghouse develop the universal electrical system, and this development led to his most successful business.

   _____

Lesson 6 Pronoun Reference Problems   *Application*

A. Eliminating Pronoun Reference Problem

Revise the sentences below to correct all indefinite, general, or ambiguous pronoun reference problems. More than one interpretation may be possible.

1. Vera jogs because it keeps her trim.

_____

2. I heard them say on the radio that the earth's climate may be changing.

_____

3. Magma forms deep within the earth, and when its crust breaks, it erupts.

_____

4. Ungulates are mammals with hoofs; this includes horses and llamas.

_____

5. It says in the recipe that rhubarb is a fruit, but it is really a plant stalk.

_____

B. Using Clear Pronoun References

In the following paragraph, find five sentences with indefinite, general, or ambiguous pronoun references. Revise the sentences on the lines below.

(1) I think I would have liked to have been an inventor—but in the old days, not now. (2) By now they've already invented all the good stuff. (3) And if I wanted to be an inventor in modern times, you would have to know too much about electronics, calculus, physics, and other sciences. (4) I don't want to spend my life in classes! (5) To be perfectly honest, I don't think I could ever have invented a computer. (6) But I could have invented some of the more basic things—the pulley, the inclined plane, maybe even the wheel. (7) Which is what really benefits the human race. (8) Logical, straightforward things—that's what I'd be good at. (9) I often think about this, which is sad. (10) I think I was born too late.

_____

_____

_____

_____

_____

_____

_____

CHAPTER 6

Name _____ Date _____

Using Adjectives and Adverbs

Teaching

Modifiers are words that describe or give more specific information about the meanings of other words. Modifiers may function as adjectives or adverbs.

Adjectives modify nouns and pronouns. They answer the questions *which one* (*that, this*), *what kind* (*blue, cool*), *how many* (*three, several*), and *how much* (*some, none*).

Words classified as other parts of speech can also function as adjectives.

NOUNS	<u>circus</u> tent
POSSESSIVE NOUNS AND PRONOUNS	<u>Shawn's</u> drums, <u>our</u> town
INDEFINITE PRONOUNS	<u>every</u> performer
DEMONSTRATIVE PRONOUNS	<u>that</u> elephant
PARTICIPLES	<u>trained</u> monkeys, <u>cheering</u> crowds
NUMBERS	<u>three</u>, <u>35</u>

Adverbs modify verbs, adjectives, and other adverbs. They answer the questions *when, where, how,* and *to what extent.*

WHEN?	The circus train arrived <u>today</u>.
WHERE?	Look <u>up</u> to see the trapeze artists.
HOW?	The crowd gathered <u>expectantly</u>.
TO WHAT EXTENT?	The animals were <u>extremely</u> well trained.

Identifying Adjectives and Adverbs

Identify the boldfaced word as an adjective or an adverb. Write **ADJ** or **ADV** on the line.

1. "Come one, come all to the greatest show on Earth!" shouts the **enthusiastic** announcer at the circus. _____

2. The spectacle **now** known as the circus began thousands of years ago. _____

3. Roman games, which were similar to today's circuses, focused **mainly** on animal acts and daring horseback riding. _____

4. During the Middle Ages, jugglers and tightrope walkers **skillfully** performed on street corners. _____

5. **Those** performers also performed before the royalty of Europe in organized shows. _____

6. Modern circuses began in England in the 1700s when Philip Astley began a show of trick **horseback** riding accompanied by live music, all within a circular structure. _____

7. American showmen **soon** began to imitate Astley's Circus, adding more acts. _____

8. In the late 1700s, circuses began exhibiting **exotic** animals. _____

9. One of these **traveling** circuses was owned by P. T. Barnum, a famous showman. _____

10. At first, horse-drawn wagons **slowly** carried the circus from town to town. _____

CHAPTER 7

Lesson 1

Using Adjectives and Adverbs   *More Practice*

A. Identifying Adjectives and the Words They Modify

Underline the adjective once and the word it modifies twice in each of the following sentences. Ignore articles and proper nouns.

1. Circus audiences loved the high-wire act of the Great Wallendas.

2. This daring family of tightrope walkers put on an amazing show for decades.

3. Their famous act was their seven-person pyramid.

4. In this act, four men walked on the wire with a steel rod connecting them.

5. On the connecting rod stood two more men; another steel rod connected them, too.

6. At the very top of the pyramid was a young woman on a chair that rested on the second rod.

7. Their act, which was always performed without a safety net, may have been the most dangerous stunt in the history of the circus.

8. Different members of the extended family took part in this incredible feat over the years.

9. Unfortunately, the act had more than its fair share of disastrous results.

10. For example, in 1962, in the middle of the act, one member of the famous troupe lost his balance, and the whole pyramid collapsed.

11. Two members were killed and one was paralyzed for life in that tragic fall.

B. Identifying Adverbs and the Words They Modify

Underline the word modified by each boldfaced adverb. Then in the blank after each sentence, identify the part of speech of the modified word. Write **V** for verb, **ADJ** for adjective, or **ADV** for adverb.

Never look **directly** at the sun during an eclipse. _____V_____

1. An **extremely** strong wind overturned the park bench. _____

2. "I **never** could do that!" exclaimed Helen. _____

3. The firefighter moved **very** cautiously through the blackened building. _____

4. We searched **everywhere** for the missing photos. _____

5. Hank drove **more** slowly as we continued up the winding road. _____

6. As we reached the stadium, we gasped at the **unusually** large crowd of fans waiting in line. _____

7. The small, **barely** red strawberries were not ripe enough to pick. _____

8. Please go to the library **now** for the information you need. _____

9. After he completed the first problem, he worked the next one **much** faster. _____

10. Marta jogs two miles **daily** in any weather. _____

CHAPTER 7

Lesson 1 # Using Adjectives and Adverbs   *Application*

A. Writing Subjects and Predicates

Complete each of the following sentences by writing an adjective or an adverb in the blank. Then write **ADJ** or **ADV** on the line to identify your word.

1. Transporting an entire circus from city to city is a
   _____ task.   _____

2. Smaller circuses, which travel by truck, give _____
   performances within a certain area.   _____

3. They may perform in a different city _____ every day.   _____

4. _____ performer and worker pitches in where needed.   _____

5. Ringling Brothers and Barnum & Bailey uses railroad cars to travel
   _____ distances.   _____

6. There are _____ units, a Red and a Blue, which follow
   their own routes.   _____

7. Each unit puts on _____ performances with plenty of
   clowns, wild animals, and other acts.   _____

8. Behind the scenes, the performers live in a _____
   organized environment.   _____

9. The circus _____ has a community kitchen, medical
   facilities, and a post office.   _____

10. The circus workers and performers live together _____
    closely, and this closeness makes them feel more like a family than a business. _____

B. Writing with Adjectives and Adverbs

Often, music concerts of today are as spectacular as the circus used to be.
Performers still try to dazzle and amaze audiences with special effects and lighting.
On the lines below, describe a live concert by a popular singer or band. You could
choose to describe the audience, the hall, or the performers themselves. Use at
least six adjectives and six adverbs in your description.

_____

_____

_____

_____

_____

_____

<table>
<tr><td>Lesson 2</td></tr>
</table>

Using Comparisons

Teaching

Use modifiers to compare things. There are three forms, or degrees, of comparison.

Degrees of Comparisons		
Base Form	describes one person, thing, or action	This park is <u>popular.</u>
Comparative	compares two	This park is <u>more</u> popular than that one.
Superlative	compares three or more	This park is the <u>most</u> popular of all.

Form the comparative or superlative of most one-syllable and two-syllable words by adding -er and -est (*sharper, sharpest*). Form the comparative or superlative form of modifiers that sound awkward with -er and -est by combining the basic form with the words *more* and *most* (*more tired, most tired*). Form the comparative or superlative of most modifiers with three syllables and those that end in -ly by using *more* and *most* (*more beautiful, most beautiful*). To make a negative comparison, use the words *less* and *least* (*less possible, least possible*).

Some familiar modifiers have irregular comparative and superlative forms: *good, better, best; bad, worse, worst; well, better, best; many, more, most; much, more, most.*

A. Identifying Comparative and Superlative Modifiers

On the line, label the boldfaced modifier **B** for base form, **C** for comparative, or **S** for superlative.

1. Each year, a **greater** number of people visit our nation's parklands than before. _____

2. Yellowstone, the world's **oldest** national park, attracts thousands of
visitors yearly. _____

3. Campers, hikers, and photographers flock to see the park's **magnificent** scenery. _____

4. Possibly the **most unusual** of the park's attractions are the bubbling
pools of mud called *mudpots*. _____

5. The park has a **large** group of geysers. _____

6. Old Faithful, which erupts on an average of every 73 minutes,
is the **most famous.** _____

7. People also come to see the park's animals since Yellowstone
is the **largest** wildlife preserve in the country. _____

B. Using Modifiers in Comparisons

Study the boldfaced modifier in each of the following sentences. If the form of the comparison is correct, write **Correct** on the line. If it is incorrect, write the correct form.

1. Over the last few years, my family has visited **many** national parks. _____

2. I think the parks in Utah are the **more beautiful** of all. _____

3. The rock formations in Bryce Canyon are **most unusual** than
those in any other park. _____

Lesson 2 # Using Comparisons   *More Practice*

A. Using Comparisons

Underline the correct form of comparison for each sentence.

1. The styles of the classical order of Greek architecture vary from the simple Doric to the much (more elegant, most elegant) Ionic and Corinthian.

2. Of the three styles, the Doric is the (earliest, earlier) and the (less elaborate, least elaborate).

3. The three styles can be distinguished, in part, by the relative complexity of their capital—the upper part of the column: the Doric capital is rather (simple, simpler) and unadorned; the Ionic capital is more elaborate; and the Corinthian capital, decorated with carvings of leaves, is the (more complexly designed, most complexly designed) of all.

4. The Corinthian style, the (more decorative, most decorative) of the three, can be observed in the ruins of Corinth near Athens, Greece.

5. Many people consider the magnificent Parthenon, with its row of 46 Doric columns, to be the (better, best) of all classical Greek temples.

6. Set on the Acropolis and built entirely of marble, the Parthenon is one of the world's (more beautiful, most beautiful) buildings.

B. Using Modifiers in Comparisons

After each sentence, write the comparative or superlative form of the word in parentheses, choosing the form that is appropriate for that sentence.

1. This is the (bad) traffic I have ever seen on this road. _____

2. Dan speaks Spanish the (fluently) in the class. _____

3. The sheriff's department uses bloodhounds that can detect even the (faint) scents. _____

4. Wallis greedily grabbed the (large) piece of cake on the plate. _____

5. That auctioneer manages to speak (rapidly) than I thought was possible. _____

6. No one on the track team runs (fast) than Ryan. _____

7. *Pepperoni Plus* is the restaurant that serves the (good) pizza in town. _____

8. The director reminded the cast to speak (distinctly) than they had in the previous rehearsal. _____

9. The detective needed a (complete) description of the suspect than I could provide. _____

10. The planet Venus appears (bright) than many stars. _____

Lesson 2

Using Comparisons

Application

A. Using Comparisons in Sentences

Write sentences comparing the following items by using the comparative or superlative form of the modifier in parentheses.

> **EXAMPLE** one doll compared to another (lifelike)
> *This doll is more lifelike than that one.*

1. weather today compared to yesterday (bad)

_____

2. one hiking trail compared to two others (difficult)

_____

3. one debater compared to three others (logically)

_____

4. one piece of candy compared to another (sweet)

_____

5. your health today compared to your health yesterday (well)

_____

6. one painting compared to another (lovely)

_____

B. Using Comparisons in Writing

Imagine that you are hiking a mountain trail with your dog or with a companion. Choose five of the words in the list below, and use their comparative and/or superlative forms in a paragraph describing your hike. Underline the words from the list that you have used.

energetic	brightly	good	lovely	quiet
slowly	tired	steep	high	delicious
hazardous	carefully	lazily	playfully	clumsy

_____

_____

_____

_____

_____

_____

_____

_____

CHAPTER 7

Problems with Comparisons

Teaching

Lesson 3

Double Comparisons Do not use both *-er* and *more* to form the comparative. Do not use both *-est* and *most* to form the superlative.

NONSTANDARD	Your cat is even more fussier than mine.
STANDARD	Your cat is even fussier than mine.

Illogical Comparisons Use the word *other* or *else* to compare an individual member with the rest of the group.

NONSTANDARD	My cat has a better pedigree than any cat.
STANDARD	My cat has a better pedigree than any other cat.

Incomplete Comparisons When you make a compound comparison, use *than* or *as* after the first modifier to avoid an incomplete comparison.

NONSTANDARD	Siamese cats are more popular in our neighborhood.
STANDARD	Siamese cats are more popular in our neighborhood than Persians.

State both parts of a comparison fully if you suspect readers are likely to misunderstand your sentence.

NONSTANDARD	I like my cat more than you.
STANDARD	I like my cat more than you like it.

A. Using Comparisons Correctly

Choose and underline the correct modifier in each sentence.

1. Although dogs and cats are both popular pets, cats tend to have the (more independent, more independenter) nature.

2. Cats have a (more keener, keener) sense of balance than many other animals.

3. They can see (better, more better) in dim light than people do.

4. Cats have the reputation of being one of the (most curious, most curiousest) members of the animal kingdom.

5. The ancient Egyptians considered the cat to be one of the (most sacred, most sacredest) of all creatures.

6. Today, many people choose the cat as their (favoritest, most favorite) pet of all.

B. Using Comparisons Logically

In each pair of sentences, choose the sentence that uses modifiers logically and clearly. Underline that sentence.

1. **a.** The whale shark is larger than any other fish.
   b. The whale shark is larger than any fish.

2. **a.** Our class decided it liked Robert Frost better.
   b. Our class decided it liked Robert Frost better than any other American poet.

3. **a.** Mr. Medeiros praised the cast more than you.
   b. Mr. Medeiors praised the cast more than you praised them.

4. **a.** For me, chemistry was a more challenging class.
   b. For me, chemistry was a more challenging class than biology.

Lesson 3

Problems with Comparisons

More Practice

A. Using Comparisons Correctly

Choose and underline the correct modifier in each sentence.

1. The *Domesday Book* is the (earliest, most earliest) census taken in England.

2. Sir Gawain, a knight of King Arthur's Round Table, was the (oldest, most oldest), of four brothers; he was also King Arthur's nephew.

3. This movie is (scarier, more scarier) the first time you see it than it is the second time.

4. If we get to the concert any (more later, later), we might as well just stay home.

5. This joke is (funnier, more funnier) when you can see the comedian's expressions.

B. Correcting Double Comparisons and Illogical and Incomplete Comparisons

Rewrite each sentence to make the comparisons clear and correct.

1. Some people think that long-haired cats are more beautiful.

   _____

2. The Persian is the most popularest of the long-haired cats.

   _____

3. The most largest cat is the Maine coon cat.

   _____

4. The Angora breed is older.

   _____

5. Siamese tend to be more vocal than any cat.

   _____

6. The Manx has back legs that are more longer than its front legs.

   _____

7. Abyssinians have more melodic voices than any cats.

   _____

8. Kittens who have been handled frequently by their owners have fewer behavior problems than any kittens.

   _____

   _____

9. These kittens learn faster.

   _____

10. Cat lovers throughout the world show their most finest cats at shows.

    _____

CHAPTER 7

Lesson 3

Problems with Comparisons

Application

A. Proofreading for Comparison Errors

The following paragraph contains several errors involving comparisons. Rewrite each sentence that uses double comparisons, illogical comparisons, or incomplete comparisons on the corresponding line below. If the sentence has no comparison errors, write **Correct** on the line.

(1) James Herriot was one of the most belovedest veterinarians in England. (2) He took care of more farm animals than any kind of animal. (3) But he said that cats were one of the most importantest reasons he became a vet. (4) He wrote many stories, including one about a cat named Alfred who was more dignified than any cat. (5) Another story was about Oscar who was more social than any of the other cats in town. (6) One of his bestest stories was about an orphaned kitten that found a home on Christmas Day. (7) And there was Moses, a cat who was more comfortable around pigs than other cats. (8) Mr. Herriot's stories are some of the most delightful cat stories ever written.

1. _____

2. _____

3. _____

4. _____

5. _____

6. _____

7. _____

8. _____

B. Using Comparisons in Writing

Imagine that you have just visited the zoo and spent a while observing the big cats—the tigers, the lions, the leopards, or the panthers. Describe the way they looked and sounded and how they moved. Use at least three comparative and three superlative modifiers, either adjectives or adverbs. Write your description on the lines below.

_____

_____

_____

_____

_____

_____

CHAPTER 7

Lesson 4

Other Modifier Problems

Teaching

Avoid these common modifier errors.

This, that, these, and *those* are **demonstrative pronouns** used as adjectives. They must agree in number with the words they modify (nonstandard: *these* kind of garbage). *Here* and *there* are never used with demonstrative adjectives (nonstandard: *this here* truck). *Them* is never used as an adjective in place of *these* or *those* (nonstandard: *them* cans).

Two pairs of words—*good* and *well*, *bad* and *badly*—can cause special problems. Study these models of correct uses.

Good adjective and predicate adjective—describes a condition
Recycling is a <u>good</u> idea.   I feel <u>good</u> when I recycle.
Well (predicate adjective or adverb)
I feel <u>well</u> now that I can breathe fresh air.   The program is working <u>well</u>.
Bad adjective and predicate adjective—describes a condition
Pollution is a <u>bad</u> problem.   We feel <u>bad</u> about our behavior.

A **misplaced modifier** is a word or phrase placed so far away from the word it modifies that the meaning of the sentence is unclear or incorrect.

CONFUSING   I glimpsed a rat <u>sorting the recyclable materials</u>.
CLEARER   <u>Sorting the recyclable materials</u>, I glimpsed a rat.

A **dangling modifier** is a word or phrase that does not clearly modify any noun or pronoun in a sentence.

MISLEADING   Speaking tirelessly to community groups, the recycling program was
             successful.
CLEARER   Speaking tirelessly to community groups, recycling promoters made the
             program a success.

Avoid using **double negatives**—two negatives in a sentence (nonstandard: *She doesn't ask for no reward.*) The words *never, hardly, barely,* and *scarcely* are considered negative.

Using the Correct Modifier

In each pair of sentences, underline the sentence that uses modifiers correctly.

1. **a.** Placed at curbside, the drivers picked up the recycled items.
   b. Placed at curbside, the recycled items were picked up by the drivers.

2. **a.** Remember to use them recycling baskets!
   b. Remember to use those recycling baskets!

3. **a.** The people of the town are cooperating well at recycling, but I'm sure they could be doing better.
   b. The people of the town are cooperating good at recycling, but I'm sure they could be doing better.

4. **a.** The speaker showed examples of items during her presentation that could not be recycled.
   b. During her presentation, the speaker showed examples of items that could not be recycled.

CHAPTER 7

Other Modifier Problems

Lesson 4

More Practice

A. Using the Correct Modifier

Underline the correct word in parentheses in each sentence.

1. After a long hike in the hot sun, a cool drink tastes especially (good, well).
2. James Michener collected (them, those) Japanese woodblock prints.
3. Judy didn't divulge the sensitive information to (no one, anyone).
4. Angela feels (bad, badly) that she cannot accept the athletic scholarship.
5. (Them, These) bruised apples were (bad, badly) packed in the crate.
6. The Neanderthals (didn't know nothing, knew nothing) of metals.
7. Don't leave the hospital until you are (real, really) well.
8. (These, This) type of newspaper is more popular than (those, that) type.
9. Our lawn doesn't (never, ever) grow (good, well) unless we fertilize it.
10. Absorbed in the poems of *A Book of Americans*, Jennifer (was scarcely, wasn't scarcely) aware of her surroundings.

B. Using Modifiers Correctly

Rewrite each sentence to make it clearer and less confusing.

1. Reading the book, the characters seemed real to her.

   _____

2. Costing over $200, the PTA donated a printer to our class.

   _____

3. As a person who values comfort above all, the too-small shoes bothered Patrice.

   _____

4. Remembering today's game at the last minute, their soccer equipment was hastily thrown in the trunk of the car.

   _____

5. Flying overhead, I saw the geese pass by in a *V*-formation.

   _____

6. Mesmerized by the approaching headlights, the car bore down upon the motionless deer.

   _____

Lesson 4

Other Modifier Problems

Application

A. Using Adjectives and Adverbs Correctly

Write sentences in which you use correctly the adjectives and adverbs given.

1. good (predicate adjective) _____

2. well (adverb) _____

3. well (predicate adjective) _____

4. bad (adjective) _____

5. bad (predicate adjective) _____

6. badly (adverb) _____

B. Writing with Adjectives and Adverbs

The following paragraph has several errors involving modifiers. Read each sentence and decide if it has an error. If it does, rewrite it correctly on the corresponding line below. If it is correct, write **Correct** on the corresponding line.

Most of us ignore crucial conservation issues that affect our lives. **(1)** For example, every week millions of newspapers are produced from thousands of trees that are never recycled. **(2)** Such misuse of that there natural resource—timber—makes no sense. After all, trees provide us with paper, wood, fruits, shade, and natural beauty. **(3)** Preventing flooding, soil erosion is controlled by the trees, too. **(4)** Releasing oxygen, life is sustained on our planet. **(5)** Unfortunately, deforestation is taking place at an alarming rate, contributing to air pollution. **(6)** Deforestation also affects the problem of global warming. **(7)** Climbing two to six degrees a year, Earth's climates may be changing. **(8)** We can do our part to preserve our forests and our planet by reducing paper usage and recycling.

1. _____

2. _____

3. _____

4. _____

5. _____

6. _____

7. _____

8. _____

CHAPTER 7

Name _____   Date _____

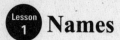

Lesson 1 ## Names   *Teaching*

Follow these rules of capitalization:

- Capitalize proper nouns and proper adjectives used alone and in compound words. *Examples:* Asia, Asian, Asian-American

  Do not capitalize prefixes such as *pre-, non-, anti-,* and *sub-* when they are joined with proper nouns and adjectives. *Example:* sub-Saharan

- Capitalize names and initials of persons. *Example:* Susan B. Anthony

- Capitalize the abbreviations *Jr.* and *Sr.,* which fall after a person's name.

- Capitalize titles and the abbreviations of titles used with personal names and in direct address. *Example:* Gen. Grant; What is your opinion, Mayor?

  Do not capitalize a title when it follows a person's name or when it is used alone. *Example:* Barbara Anderson, professor of computer science, will speak.

- Capitalize abbreviations of titles when they follow names. *Example:* Lee Ames, Ph. D.

  Do not capitalize the prefix *ex-,* the suffix *–elect,* or the words *former* or *late* when used with a title. *Example:* ex-Governor Williams

- Capitalize words indicating family relationships only when they are used as parts of names or in direct address. *Example:* Aunt Irene

  Do not capitalize family names preceded by articles or possessive words. *Example:* my uncle

Capitalizing Names

Underline the letters that should be capitalized in each of the following sentences. If the sentence is already correct, write **Correct.**

1. I am researching martin luther king, jr., for my history project. _____

2. Jim thorpe, an all-american football player and winner of two Olympic gold medals, was a native american of the sac-fox tribe. _____

3. Speaking russian fluently, the secretary of state greeted the russian diplomat. _____

4. The english courtier, navigator, and historian sir walter raleigh was an example of gallantry for people around the world. _____

5. The initials in writer s. n. behrman's name stand for samuel nathaniel. _____

6. Our family gathering at Thanksgiving includes grandma and grandpa Castillo, aunt dorothy, and uncle ted. _____

7. Governor-elect Richards is conferring with her most trusted associate, G. R. Trenton. _____

8. czech dramatist karel capek introduced the word *robot* to the english language. _____

9. My cousin Jeannie is proud of the italian-made shoes and the french perfume she purchased on a trip to Europe. _____

10. What has the space probe into the Venusian atmosphere uncovered, Professor? _____

CHAPTER 8

Lesson 1

Names

More Practice

A. Capitalizing Names

Underline the letters that should be capitals in each of the following sentences. If the sentence is already correct, write **Correct**.

1. Luis j. castaneda, jr. was chosen by fellow latin-americans for an award. _____

2. My grandmother found the thai herbs and spices she wanted at the asian food store. _____

3. The pre-Raphaelite painters were actually English and lived many years after the Italian painter Raphael's death. _____

4. The noted explorer adm. Richard e. byrd made several trips to Antarctica. _____

5. May we have your comments, governor, on the new tax bill just passed by the Senate? _____

6. Lisa wilcox, d.d.s., director of the dental clinic, has written a comprehensive book on orthodontics. _____

7. At state university the new library will be named in honor of the late dean pitt. _____

8. Mother and Father invited Aunt Beth and Uncle Tim to their condominium in Myrtle Beach. _____

9. When she traveled to Washington, d.c., grandmother taylor visited the Smithsonian's air and space museum. _____

10. Our librarian, Ms. Steele, read several selections by Robert W. Service, a poet who often wrote about the Yukon. _____

B. Capitalizing Correctly

Underline each lowercase letter that should be capitalized in the following paragraph.

    (1) The first group to reach the South Pole was led by a norwegian explorer, roald amundsen. **(2)** amundsen was born in 1872 near oslo, norway. **(3)** He briefly thought of becoming a doctor, but soon became more interested in exploration, especially in the arctic and antarctic regions. **(4)** In 1898, he overwintered in antarctic waters aboard the ship *Belgica*, the first ship to do so. **(5)** In January, 1911, amundsen and his party landed at the eastern edge of the Ross Ice Shelf. **(6)** He and his crew found themselves in competition with an english expedition to the South Pole led by robert f. scott. **(7)** The following spring amundsen's crew began their overland journey at the scheduled time, while scott's expedition was unable to get underway because of bad weather. **(8)** amundsen's party reached the South Pole on December 14, leaving a tent and a norwegian flag as proof of their achievement. **(9)** Tragically, scott's party, after reaching the South Pole, all died on their way back to base camp.

Lesson 1 Names

A. Proofreading

Proofread the following first draft of a report. Look especially for errors in capitalization. Draw three lines under each letter that should be capitalized. Draw a slash through any letter that is capitalized when it should be lowercased.

EXAMPLE For *Centuries* a crippling disease affected thousands of victims, including *president franklin d. roosevelt.*

In the 1950s, polio, a crippling disease caused by a virus, caused much suffering. An american researcher, dr. jonas e. salk, provided a ray of hope by developing the first vaccine to prevent this illness. Salk, the eldest of three Sons, was born in New York City in 1914. His Father worked in the low-paying garment industry, so young salk financed his education through Scholarships and working after school. He graduated from New York University School of Medicine, where he had begun research on viruses with thomas francis, jr. Following francis to the University of Michigan, salk became an Assistant Professor. He and francis worked on developing Influenza vaccines as well as on the mass testing of the polio vaccine. Salk, his Wife, and Sons were among the first to receive the vaccine. For his efforts, salk received many honors, including a citation from president dwight d. eisenhower.

B. Writing with Capital Letters

Write a short speech to introduce a speaker to an audience. Include at least five names, using the guidelines described in this lesson. Include at least one proper noun, one proper adjective, one name with *Jr.* or *Sr.*, and an abbreviation of a title following the person's name. Be sure to capitalize correctly.

_____

_____

_____

_____

_____

_____

_____

_____

_____

_____

Other Names and Places
Teaching

Follow these rules of capitalization:

- Capitalize the names of ethnic groups, races, languages, and nationalities, as well as adjectives formed from these names. *Examples:* Peruvian, Navajo

- Capitalize all names referring to religions and their followers, sacred days and writings, and deities. *Examples:* Catholic; Yom Kippur; Islam

  Do not capitalize the words *god* and *goddess* in reference to ancient mythology.

- Capitalize the names of specific places, such as cities or states (Phoenix, Arizona); regions (the West); countries (England); parts of the world (Africa); land features (the Rockies); bodies of water (the Black Sea); and streets and highways (Division Street, Route 66).

  Do not capitalize words that refer to locations and general directions of the compass. *Example:* I live six miles west of downtown.

- Capitalize the names of historical events (French and Indian War); historical periods (Enlightenment); and calendar items, such as days, months, and holidays. Do not capitalize the names of the seasons.

Capitalizing Names and Places

Underline the words that should be capitalized in each of the following sentences. If the item is capitalized correctly, write **Correct** on the line.

1. Giotto, an Italian artist of the renaissance, painted religious frescoes. _____

2. To commemorate the end of the civil war, Congress set aside a special holiday called the day of rejoicing. _____

3. The most recent of the ice ages occurred during the period known as the pleistocene epoch. _____

4. In the civil war, the battles of bull run were fought on july 21, 1861, and august 29-30, 1962, near the town of manassas in virginia. _____

5. Tony's great-grandfather often talks about the hardships of life during the Great Depression of the 1930s. _____

6. Before driving on to the states of the west last summer, the Kirks followed the mississippi river south. _____

7. During world war II, Eddie Rickenbacker was forced down in the pacific ocean about 600 miles north of the island of samoa, but he was eventually rescued. _____

8. On a trip to germany, Marvin took a boat trip on the rhine river and spent a week in bavaria, going by cable car to germany's highest mountain, the zugspitze. _____

9. venus was the roman goddess of love and mars was the god of war. _____

10. What do you know about the followers of Hinduism and Islam? _____

Lesson 2

Other Names and Places

More Practice

A. Capitalizing Names and Places

Underline the words that should be capitalized in each of the following sentences. If the sentence is capitalized correctly, write *correct* in the margin.

1. In Greek mythology the gods and goddesses have supernatural powers but possess human qualities as well.

2. Greek myths had their origin in the stories of the ancient mycenaean and dorian civilizations.

3. To explain the source of evil in the world, the greeks invented the myth of Pandora's box.

4. The rising and setting of the sun was interpreted as the god helios driving his chariot across the sky from east to west.

5. Poseidon was known as the Ruler of the Sea (the mediterranean sea).

6. The god zeus cast lightning bolts on his enemies from his palace on mount olympus in northern greece.

7. Both the ancient greeks and the maoris of new zealand related similar stories of the separation of the earth and sky.

8. Some Greek gods and goddesses were associated with certain cities; thus, the people of delphi worshipped apollo, while the citizens of athens adored athena.

9. When was the fabled Golden Age of Greek culture?

10. Every five years a great fall festival was held in september to honor the goddess of corn, demeter.

B. Capitalizing Names of Places in a Paragraph

Draw three lines under each letter that should be capitalized in the following paragraph.

Istanbul is turkey's largest city and the only major metropolis to lie on two continents. The bosporus strait, which connects the black sea and the sea of marmara, divides istanbul. Thus, part of the city is in asia and part is in europe. Istanbul, formerly known as constantinople, is an old city. From the fourth to the 15th century, it served as the capital of the byzantine empire. It then became the seat of the ottoman empire until the early 20th century. Tourists enjoy visiting the enormous covered bazaar and topkapi palace, a museum which was once the home of turkish sultans. Famous religious buildings include the islamic sultan ahmet mosque and the impressive christian cathedral, hagia sophia, built by emperor justinian in the sixth century.

CHAPTER 8

Lesson 2

Other Names and Places

Application

A. Proofreading for Capital Letters

Read the following advertisement for a tour that includes these centers of religion: Rome and Jerusalem. Draw three lines under any letters that should be capitalized but are not. Draw a slash across any letter that is capitalized incorrectly.

EXAMPLE Imagine the *Trip* of a lifetime to sites of religious significance in europe and asia.

Join Spirit Tours for 14 days of unforgettable experiences in rome and jerusalem. We arrive in rome on sunday, just in time to visit the world's largest christian Church, the Basilica of Saint Peter. While in vatican city we will tour the magnificent Sistine Chapel and view the ceiling paintings by that renowned renaissance artist, michelangelo. We'll have time to shop on that bustling street, the via veneto, and to sample sumptuous italian cuisine at the many fine restaurants near the tiber river. On friday we jet East to jerusalem, just in time for the muslim sabbath. We will visit the holiest muslim shrine, the Dome of the Rock. Nearby we will see the ancient Wailing Wall, sacred to the jews as the only remnant of the temple built by solomon. Later we will tour other sites revered by christians.

B. Capitalizing Names of Places

You probably know a great deal about your neighborhood and city. You know where stores, places of worship, restaurants, and other attractions are located. Pretend you are introducing a stranger to your city. Write a description of a few of the places that he or she should not miss. Include general directions about how to get to each location.

_____

_____

_____

_____

_____

_____

_____

_____

CHAPTER 8

Lesson 3 — Organizations and Other Subjects   *Teaching*

Use capital letters for the following:

- All important words in the names of organizations, businesses, teams, institutions, government bodies, and political parties. *Examples:* Woodview City Council, Justrite Corporation, Springdale Hospital, Congress, Democratic Party

  Don't capitalize words such as *democratic, republican, socialist,* or *communist* when they refer to principles or forms of government.

- Names of stars, planets, galaxies, constellations, and other specific objects in the universe. *Examples:* Ursa Major, Pluto, Milky Way (but not sun and moon)

  Do not capitalize *earth* when it is preceded by the article *the*.

- Names of specific ships, trains, airplanes, cars, and spacecraft. *Example: Voyager II*

- Names of monuments, memorials, and other landmarks. *Example:* Lincoln Memorial

- Names of school subjects only when they refer to specific courses. Capitalize proper nouns and adjectives that are part of these names. *Examples:* Medieval Poetry I, gym, drafting

- Capitalize the words *freshman, sophomore, junior,* and *senior* only when they are part of a proper noun. *Example:* Senior Prom

- Capitalize the names of awards, special events, and brand names. Do not capitalize a common noun following a brand name. *Examples:* Centennial Celebration, Super Soy hot dogs

Identifying Correct Capitalization

Underline the words or letters that should be capitals in each of the following sentences. (One sentence is already capitalized correctly.)

1. Jack plans to take four summer courses: latin, music 201, english, and math.

2. The earth has one satellite, the moon; but mars has two, phobos and deimos.

3. Our new cologne, enigma, should be available to consumers by this fall.

4. All seniors will meet on Friday to learn more about the carlin award.

5. The north star, also called polaris, is visible over the northern hemisphere.

6. In 1973, the U.S. *mariner ix* became the first spacecraft to orbit mars; in 1974, the *mariner x* became the first spacecraft to fly past two planets—venus and mercury.

7. The height of luxury would be to travel by rail on the *orient express* and later to sail on a cruise ship such as the *stella polaris*.

8. The better business bureau sent notices to entrepreneurs inviting them to attend the small business seminar next week.

9. Many juniors participated in the mentoring program co-sponsored by acme computer company and the department of education.

10. Generous benefactors of children's hospital held a large fundraising party at the erie monument to raise money for a new solarium.

11. The legislation easily passed in the senate since members of both the republican party and the democratic party voted for it.

12. Many communist governments fell from power in the 1990s and were replaced by new leadership eager to try a more democratic form of government.

Lesson 3 # Organizations and Other Subjects   *More Practice*

A. Capitalizing Names of Organizations and Other Subjects

Underline each letter that should be capitalized in the following sentences.

1. To promote our interest in physics II, our teacher provides varied experiences.
2. At the glenn research center, we learned how scientists work on problems relating to flight in the earth's atmosphere and in outer space.
3. We saw a photo of the 1994 collision between the comet shoemaker-levy 9 and jupiter, taken by the Hubble Space Telescope.
4. At the cuyahoga county office building, we examined data on structural damage to bridges caused by corrosion.
5. Then we visited the hope memorial bridge to see the preventive measures the county government had taken.
6. Our next stop was techno industries, the winner of the prestigious stein award for excellence in polymer research.
7. Their product, polycon, is used by such companies as globalwide airlines and transcontinental shipping.
8. Most of the seniors will be attending the national physics exhibition in the spring, which, we hope, will not be held at the same time as senior recognition week.

B. Capitalizing Correctly

Underline the words in each sentence that should be capitalized. Then write them correctly on the corresponding lines below. If a sentence is capitalized correctly, write **Correct**.

   (1) All juniors and seniors may take a new course, comparative government 301, beginning second semester. (2) Institutions such as parliament, congress, and the supreme court will be studied in depth. (3) The role of political parties, especially the American democratic party and republican party, will be analyzed. (4) We will study the relationship of government to world organizations, such as the united nations and the world bank. (5) Then we will explore the interaction of government with national and international businesses, particularly micromarvelous computer company, intershipping corporation, and others. (6) The course will conclude with a weeklong trip to Washington, D.C., during which we will visit such democratic shrines as the Washington Monument. (7) One full day will be spent at senate and house debates and hearings. (8) Our visit will conclude with our attendance at the presidential awards ceremony at the white house.

1. _____   5. _____
2. _____   6. _____
3. _____   7. _____
4. _____   8. _____

Organizations and Other Subjects

Application

A. Proofreading for Capitalization Errors

Read the following speech given at the awards ceremony at your high school. Draw three lines under any letters that should be capitalized but are not. Draw a slash across any letter that is capitalized in error.

EXAMPLE Welcome to the M̸eeting of the f̲i̲ne a̲r̲ts c̲ommission of Centerville.

      The fine arts commission is honored to recognize a truly special Senior for the outstanding citizen award, Demetrius Hawkins. Demetrius is directly responsible for the construction of the Minipark adjoining adler children's hospital. Not only did he persuade midvale city council to donate the land, he also persuaded major landscaping to contribute several trees and shrubs. Then he convinced the midvale high school hawks and the botany 101 class to plant the flowers and grass. On behalf of mayor standish, we present this Plaque, a replica of the statue of liberty, to Demetrius. Furthermore, by unanimous agreement of the centerville city council, the Minipark is hereby named Hawkins park.

B. Using Capitalization in Writing

Write a speech to be given on graduation day in an imaginary high school somewhere in your state. Try to predict the futures of some of the members of the graduating class. (Do not name real people. Use imaginary names.) Be sure to use capital letters correctly in your paragraph. Include names from the following categories:

    a college or university   a landmark or a monument
    a business or institution   an award
    a political party   a school subject

_____

_____

_____

_____

_____

_____

_____

_____

_____

_____

_____

Lesson 4

First Words and Titles

Teaching

Capitalize the following words:

- Capitalize the first words of every sentence and of every line of traditional poetry.
- Capitalize when quoting fewer than four lines poetry, use slash marks between the lines, and mimic the capitalization in the poem.
- Capitalize the first word of a direct quotation, if it is a complete sentence. Do not capitalize a direct quotation if it is a sentence fragment. Do not capitalize the first word of the second part of a quotation unless it starts a new sentence. *Example:* "Cowards," said William Shakespeare, "die many times before their deaths."
- Capitalize the first word of each item in an outline and the letters that introduce major subsections.
- Capitalize the first word in the greeting of a letter, the word *Sir* or *Madam,* and the first word of the closing.
- Capitalize the pronoun *I.*
- Capitalize the first, last, and all other important words in titles, including verbs, but not conjunctions, articles, or prepositions with fewer than five letters unless they begin the title.

Capitalizing First Words and Titles

Underline the words that should be capitalized in each of the following items.

1. "we will be reading William Shakespeare's tragedy *hamlet* this semester," said Ms. Young.

2. "last year," volunteered one student, "we read his comedy *the merchant of venice.*"

3. the quality of mercy is not strain'd, / it droppeth as the gentle rain from heaven
   —William Shakespeare, *The Merchant of Venice*

4. I. shakespeare's tragedies
   a. *hamlet*   b. *king lear*
   II. shakespeare's comedies
   a. *all's well that ends well*   b. *as you like it*

5. i remember that Shylock demanded a "pound of flesh" as payment for a debt.

6. "this year," said Mrs. Young, "you will leave the streets of Venice behind and will go to the cold, bleak home of the 'melancholy Dane' Hamlet."

7. i am sure you have heard this quote from *hamlet*: "to be, or not to be: that is the question."

8. "has anyone here ever read the play *romeo and juliet*?" asked Mrs. Young. "has anyone ever seen the movie?"

9. "many people feel that Shakespeare's words are as relevant today as they were during the 1500s," said Ms. Young.

10. This above all: to thine own self be true,
    and it must follow, as the night the day.
    thou canst not then be false to any man.
    —William Shakespeare, *Hamlet*

First Words and Titles

More Practice

A. Capitalizing First Words and Titles

In the following sentences underline the words that should be capitalized but are not. If the sentence contains no capitalization errors, write **Correct** on the line.

1. Una just finished reading Hofstadter's book *anti-intellectualism in american life*.

2. success is counted sweetest
   by those who ne'er succeed.
                    —Emily Dickinson

3. did you read the syndicated column called "one woman's opinion"?

4. According to the Bible, money is the "root of all evil."

5. dear ms. Rogers:
   Tonight's meeting will be at 6:00.
   yours truly,
   Helen Sims

6. "have you read *frost in may*?" asked Laurie. "it's a wonderful book."

7. Dad reads two newspapers each morning, the *bellville herald* and the local paper.

8. she is using *re-creating the past* as one of the sources for her history term paper.

9. I really enjoyed Rachel Carson's *The Sea Around Us*.

10. "This sandwich is very tasty," said Sally. "however, I'm not really hungry."

11. One of Gilbert and Sullivan's more popular operettas is *the pirates of penzance*.

12. In Eugene O'Neil's play *days without end*, two actors portray different aspects of a character's personality.

B. Capitalizing Words in Outlines

Triple underline each letter that should be capitalized in the following outline.

Selected Works of William Shakespeare

I. first period of Shakespeare's plays

   a. *the comedy of errors*

   b. *king john*

II. second period of Shakespeare's plays

   a. *julius caesar*

   b. *love's labours lost*

First Words and Titles

Application

A. Writing a Conversation

Continue this conversation by two people leaving a theater after seeing a play. Include at least four titles, as the speakers compare this play and its actors to others they have seen or read. Be sure to capitalize the quotations and titles correctly.

"I hope nobody can tell I was crying at the end of that play," Gayle said. "I was hoping that the main characters would reunite finally."

"I've got to admit, it was pretty sad," replied Alice. "But at the same time, it was too sentimental for me. I prefer plays with more humor and realism."

_____

_____

_____

_____

B. Writing an Outline Using Capital Letters Correctly

Read the following brief report. Then write a short outline for it on the lines below. Be sure to capitalize correctly.

William Shakespeare's career as a playwright is sometimes divided into three distinct periods. During the first period (1590-1594), his plays seem to be a collection of episodes, rather than one compelling story. During this period, characters' lines are written in an immature, flowery style.

During the second period (1595-1600), Shakespeare matured as a playwright and created plays of near perfection. His plots became more unified, and his characters became more realistic.

Plays of the third period (1601-1608) reflect Shakespeare's interest in tragedy over comedy. His emphasis was on creating characters of great complexity.

William Shakespeare's Playwriting Periods

_____

_____

_____

_____

_____

_____

_____

_____

_____

Lesson
5 **Abbreviations**   *Teaching*

Capitalize these abbreviations:

• abbreviations of the names of cities, states, countries, and other places.
  Examples: UT (Utah), UK (United Kingdom)

• abbreviations related to time. Examples: B.C., A.D., A.M., P.M.

• abbreviations of organizations and agencies. Examples: FBI (Federal Bureau of
  Investigation)

Capitalizing Abbreviations

Underline the letters that should be capitalized in each of the following sentences.
If the sentence is already correct, write **Correct**.

1. Professor Gearity's class on Franklin Roosevelt's administration began last night
   at exactly 7:00 p.m.

2. Before she began, she wrote on this address on the board: Warm Springs, ga.

3. What u.s. president is associated with that town in Georgia?

4. Franklin D. Roosevelt was born on January 30, a.d. 1882.

5. The Roosevelt family's ancestor Klaes Marensen Van Roosevelt had settled in
   New York City around a.d. 1640.

6. Franklin D. Roosevelt, who was also known as fdr, was elected president of the
   u.s. in 1932.

7. During his first hundred days in office, he started many programs, including the
   Agricultural Adjustment Act (aaa), which gave relief to the nation's farmers.

8. The National Recovery Act (nra) was established to fight the effects of the
   Great Depression on u.s. industries.

9. When you see the abbreviation nra today, what organization comes to mind?

10. Other programs begun by the Roosevelt administration include the Civil
    Works Administration (cwa) and the Civilian Conservation Corps, also known
    as the ccc.

11. The cwa provided funds for public projects across the u.s.

12. The ccc was a program that employed young people in projects such as
    building dams and improving public parks.

13. During Roosevelt's administration, labor unions such as the afl and the cio
    gained strength.

14. What is the significance of the Warm Springs address? fdr, 32nd president of
    the u.s., died at his home in Warm Springs on April 12, 1945.

Abbreviations

More Practice

A. Capitalizing Abbreviations

Underline the letters that should be capitals in each of the following sentences. If the sentence is already correct, write **Correct**.

1. Is the company's address Cleveland, oh, or Cleveland, tn? _____

2. The Central Intelligence Agency is more commonly referred to as the CIA. _____

3. The space shuttle is scheduled to land at 3:00 p.m. _____

4. Is Alaska's postal code al or ak? _____

5. Augustus, who became the first Roman emperor in 27 b.c., died in a.d. 14. _____

6. Does the Animal Protective League, or the apl, have a newsletter? _____

7. Will the awards ceremony for the NEA (National Endowment for the Arts) be broadcast on public television? _____

8. The last line of the address should read "Chamberlain, SD 57325." _____

9. All 12 nations in nato signed the North Atlantic Treaty on April 4, 1949, in Washington, d.c. _____

10. Plato was a Greek philosopher who was born in 428 b.c. and died in 348 b.c. _____

11. Don't call your friend in N.Y.C. at 10:00 P.M. Pacific Standard Time (pst). It's already 1:00 a.m. on the East Coast. _____

B. Capitalizing Correctly

Underline each lowercase letter that should be capitalized in the numbered sentences of the following paragraph.

Who were the greatest leaders of all time? **(1)** Some people might choose Alexander the Great, king of Macedonia around 340 b.c. His rule extended throughout much of the civilized world. **(2)** Certainly Julius Caesar, who made Rome the center of a huge empire around the year 50 b.c., would have to appear on someone's list. **(3)** Like Alexander and Julius Caesar, Napoleon Bonaparte, born in a.d. 1769, was a military genius who conquered most of Europe. But must a leader conquer others to be great? **(4)** Some people think that Franklin D. Roosevelt (fdr) was a great leader. **(5)** He instituted programs such as the National Recovery Act (nra) and the Civilian Conservation Corps (ccc) to lift the u.s. out of the economic doldrums of the Great Depression. **(6)** Would you include the framers of the United Nations (un) as some of the greatest leaders? **(7)** At the un, nations come together, not as individuals or even as members of other organizations such as nato or seato. **(8)** Instead, in organizations such as unicef, nations come together as a world family to solve problems. What great leaders would make the cut on your list?

Abstract Abbreviations

Lesson 5

Application

A. Proofreading

The following paragraph is a draft of an article about the school organizations to be printed at the beginning of the year. Before this article appears in the school newspaper, it must be proofread. Proofread the report, looking especially for errors in the capitalization of abbreviations. Draw three lines under each letter that should be capitalized.

> **EXAMPLE** If you want to learn about the clubs at Pomeroy High School
> (<u>phs</u>), come to an orientation meeting at 9:00 <u>a.m.</u> on Wednesday,
> September 15.

Pomeroy High School has a wealth of choices for students who want to become involved. For example, are you interested in national and international issues? Join the jcwa (Junior Council on World Affairs), which meets in room 15 every Tuesday at 3:30 p.m. Are you interested in being of service to the greater Pomeroy community? Learn more about the Pomeroy Service Club (psc) on Thursdays at 3:45 p.m. Early risers fascinated by computers can meet fellow computer enthusiasts at the pcc (Pomeroy Computer Club) meetings in the computer room in the library at 7:30 a.m. every other Friday. The fea (Future Educators of America) has an active chapter at the school, too. These are just a few of the clubs that would like to have you as a member. For a complete listing of school organizations, send a self-addressed, stamped envelope to this address: Pomeroy High School Clubs, 3572 School St., Pomeroy, ca 94550.

B. Writing with Capital Letters

Think of issues that you feel should be attended to by the federal or state government, such as hunger, homelessness, or crime. Then make up organizations that are responsible for those problems and abbreviate their names. Write a brief report describing the function of each of those fictional organizations. Finally, provide the fictional address of each organization.

_____

_____

_____

_____

_____

Periods and Other End Marks

Lesson 1

Teaching

Use a **period** after these sentences:

DECLARATIVE SENTENCE	The doctor will see you now.
IMPERATIVE SENTENCE	Wait in this room.
INDIRECT QUESTION	The doctor asked if anything hurt.

Use an **exclamation point** after these groups of words:

EXCLAMATORY SENTENCE	How lucky we are!
STRONG INTERJECTION	Hey!
WORDS THAT EXPRESS A SOUND	Crack!

Use a **question mark** after these sentences:

| INTERROGATIVE SENTENCE | How do you feel today? |
| DECLARATIVE SENTENCE THAT ASKS A QUESTION | She cut her finger? |

Use a period with abbreviations and initials (Examples: Rd., Jr., hr., min., ft., in.) and after each number or letter in an outline or list.

Do **not** use periods with metric measurements (Examples: cm, kg); acronyms (Examples: NATO); abbreviations pronounced letter by letter (Example: CIA); state names in postal addresses (Examples: CA, NH); or positions on a compass (N, S, E, W).

Using Periods and Other End Marks

Add periods, question marks, and exclamation points as necessary in the following items.

1. Doctors have not always known as much about the human body as they know today

2. Disease was often thought to be caused by supernatural forces

3. Around AD 1600, Dr William Harvey of England experimented and discovered that the heart pumps blood throughout the body

4. What a breakthrough that simple idea was

5. Doctors realized that, to treat disease, they had to understand the body's structure

6. Also in the 1600s, another scientist, Anton van Leeuwenhoek, discovered tiny organisms that we call germs

7. Without knowledge of germs, do you think we would understand the enormous value of cleanliness

8. We can thank two US scientists, Crawford Long and William Morton, for discovering that ether gas could safely put patients to sleep during surgery

9. Ouch Just imagine any surgery without a painkiller

10. How will medical research change our lives in the future

11. I Epidemics in Europe during the Middle Ages
    A Leprosy
    B Black Plague
    C Smallpox

CHAPTER 9

Lesson 1 **Periods and Other End Marks**   *More Practice*

A. Using End Marks

Add periods, question marks, and exclamation points where they are needed in the following sentences.

1. Wait You didn't say whether to phone at 9 AM or 9 PM
2. Rita, who has an MA in art history, works for PBS
3. Should I write *PA* or *Penn* on the envelope of a business letter
4. Is the NASA headquarters located in Washington, DC, or at Cape Canaveral, Florida
5. Her new address is PO Box 42, Mt Vernon, IL 62864
6. Wow What a ruthless character Lady Macbeth was
7. She asked what percentage of the student body belongs to SADD
8. Would you please return the enclosed form as soon as possible
9. The poet WH Auden was born in England but became a US citizen
10. Do you remember where you put the 500 ml beaker
11. Some theaters now charge $750 for a movie ticket
12. Have you read George Orwell's novel *Keep the Aspidistra Flying*
13. You bet We'd love to attend the cookout
14. He wanted to know whether I planned to attend UCLA or MIT
15. Dr Florence Brown will speak to the JCWA about health conditions in Russia
16. Pardon I couldn't hear what you were saying
17. You threw out my favorite shirt What were you thinking
18. Bang What a loud sound the starting pistol makes
19. Reliable Couriers Ltd delivers all local packages on the same day they were sent
20. The following items on your home must be repaired:
    1 leaking gutters
    2 cracks in the sidewalk

B. Using Periods in Outlines

Add periods where they are needed in the following outline.

Medicine
 I History of medicine
   A Medical progress in ancient Egypt
   B Ancient Chinese medicine
   C Medicine in ancient Greece and Rome
     1 Hippocrates
     2 Galen
 II Role of the doctor
   A Diagnosis
   B Treatment
     1 Medical treatments
     2 Surgery

Lesson 1

Periods and Other End Marks

Application

A. Proofreading

Add periods, question marks, and exclamation points where necessary in the following paragraph. To insert a question mark or exclamation point, insert a caret ⌃ and add the needed punctuation mark above the caret. To insert a period, use this symbol ⊙ at the appropriate place.

> Itzhak Perlman, the violinist from Israel, is outstanding in at least two ways First, he is an incredible musical talent; and second, he copes every day with a severe disability His disability doesn't prevent him from doing what he loves to do—play the violin When Itzhak was only four years old, he contracted polio As a result of this disease, he lost use of his legs What a blow that must have been to his parents How did the family react to the tragedy They simply concentrated on making the most of Itzhak's strengths His most obvious strength was a prodigious musical ability When Itzhak was 13 years old, he appeared on the Ed Sullivan Show on US television Imagine how excited he must have been Suddenly, the whole world knew about Itzhak Perlman and his talent Since then, he has appeared with orchestras all over the world He is also spokesman for the disabled and a constant proof that being disabled shouldn't mean giving up your dreams

B. Using End Marks in an Outline

If you were planning a trip to a distant country, such as India or Japan, what decisions and plans would you have to make? Which decisions should be made weeks or days before the trip, and which decisions would be made just prior to leaving? On the form below, outline your plans for a trip to a familiar or exotic location. Give the outline a title, and identify two major divisions, for example, long-range planning and short-range details. Then suggest three main ideas under each division. Be sure to punctuate correctly.

Title:

I _____

  A _____

  B _____

  C _____

II _____

  A _____

  B _____

  C _____

Commas in Sentence Parts

Teaching

Use commas after introductory words or mild interjections such as *no, yes, oh,* and *well;* after introductory prepositional phrases that contain additional prepositional phrases; after adverbial clauses or adverbs used as introductory elements; and after introductory infinitives or participial phrases.

> No, I haven't heard the latest weather report.
> From a report on the radio, I learned that a tornado has been sighted.
> Although I know they are dangerous, I find tornadoes exciting.
> To protect myself against the tornado, I went to the basement.
> Listening to the roar of the wind, I began to get nervous.

Use commas to set off words of direct address, such as names and titles. Use commas to set off parenthetical expressions—words that interrupt the flow of thought in a sentence—and to separate a question tagged onto a sentence at the end.

> By the way, Grace, you opened the windows a crack, didn't you?

Use commas to set off nonessential clauses and participial phrases and nonessential appositives and appositive phrases.

> My house, which doesn't have a basement, is newer than yours, an old colonial.

Use a comma before the conjunction that joins the two independent clauses of a compound sentence.

> A tornado touched down, but it skipped over our neighborhood.

In a series of three or more, use a comma after every item in the series except the last one. Use a comma between two or more adjectives of equal rank that modify the same noun.

> After the strong, unexpected storm, we surveyed our house, our yard, and our neighborhood.

Using Commas Correctly

Insert commas where necessary in the following sentences.

1. Braving the blinding snow and bitter cold I shoveled the driveway the sidewalk and the steps this morning.

2. Light the candles Reece because we lost electricity.

3. The schools are canceled today and they will probably be closed again tomorrow because of the snowstorm.

4. Well we should consider ourselves lucky that the farm suffered only minor damage from the storm.

5. Mr. Cafarella this blizzard was worse than the last one don't you agree?

6. On the contrary this storm was mild compared to the ones I lived through when I was a boy.

7. In the middle of the night I awoke because the wind was making so much noise.

8. Looking out the window I began to suspect that this was no ordinary storm.

9. The road crews which stand by when bad weather is predicted were busy all night.

10. When the wind and snow finally stopped we all came out to survey the damage.

Lesson 2

Commas in Sentence Parts

More Practice

A. Using Commas

Underline the words in each sentence that should be followed by a comma. If no commas are necessary, write **None** on the line.

1. To enjoy a period of quiet each morning Molly reads for an hour. _____

2. Mustering his courage Bill tried out for the school play. _____

3. Even wet tattered newspapers can be recycled. _____

4. My how you have grown! _____

5. Keep up the good work Brendan! _____

6. Increased use of paper products concern about pollution and
scarcity of forest land have made recycling a necessity. _____

7. At work she has no time for chatting on the phone. _____

8. The diamond one of two crystalline forms of the element carbon can
be produced synthetically. _____

9. Salty and fat-filled snacks of course should be avoided. _____

10. Abraham Lincoln's stepmother gave him the few books she owned
but she herself had never been taught to read. _____

11. Sheila put her pet into its carrier and rushed it to the vet's office
but she had to wait her turn. _____

12. The crossing guard at our street who is retired always has a friendly smile. _____

13. Yes we'd love to come over on Thanksgiving Aunt Alice. _____

14. Eventually all the runners made it to the finish line. _____

B. Using Commas in Writing

Insert commas where they are needed the following paragraphs.

Oh blizzards can cause so much trouble! Some people think a blizzard is
just a lot of snow but in a true blizzard the snow is also accompanied by very
high winds. Having survived several blizzards in my lifetime I know quite a bit
about the destruction they can cause. The high winds and heavy snow can
knock down power lines branches and trees. It can take me several hours to
shovel my driveway which is very long. After removing piles of heavy wet
snow city crews often run out of places to put it all. While I was living in a city
near the coast I learned that a blizzard usually causes ocean waves to reach
much farther inland than usual. To escape the risk of floods many people must
evacuate their homes during a blizzard. A blizzard my friend is one of the
worst types of storms. Now when you hear about blizzards in another part of
the country you won't just think of fun in the snow will you?

Lesson 2 # Commas in Sentence Parts   *Application*

A. Writing with Commas

Add commas where they are needed in the following paragraph.

It is an understatement to say that tornadoes are dangerous storms. With their winds of over 300 miles per hour tornadoes can cause amazing destruction. Spreading over hundreds of yards tornadoes may travel over land for many miles before they lose speed. Tornadoes which are also called twisters and cyclones have reduced pressure in the center of the funnel. In fact in the path of a tornado homes schools and other buildings often explode because they are not well enough ventilated to adjust to the pressure difference. Frequently tornadoes which usually form in the springtime appear in intense small-scale storms. Yes tornadoes can form over water as well. These types of tornadoes by the way are usually called waterspouts. Whenever and wherever you see a tornado take it very seriously. It can cause real damage.

B. Using Commas in Writing

Rewrite the sentences by following the directions in parentheses.

1. Joe's garage was filled with various items. (Include a series of items.)

_____

_____

2. Today was a perfect day to clean the garage. (Include two adjectives of equal rank that modify the same noun.)

_____

3. Joe carried everything into the driveway. (Add an introductory phrase or clause.)

_____

4. His mother said, "This isn't such a bad job." (Add a noun of direct address and a question tagged on the end of the sentence.)

_____

5. The family car couldn't even fit in the garage before. (Include a nonessential clause.)

_____

6. The job was finally done. It was time for dinner (Combine the sentences with a conjunction.)

_____

Fixing Comma Problems

Lesson 3

Teaching

Use a **comma** to separate words that might be misread.

> Filmmakers, say many critics, should make their films more realistic.

Use a **comma** to replace an omitted word or words.

> Many women enjoy films about relationships; men, about adventure.

Use a **comma** with antithetical phrases that make a contrast by using words such as *not* or *unlike*.

> Films, unlike plays, can be produced on location.

Use a **comma** before a coordinating conjunction (*and, but, or*) to avoid comma splice, an error that occurs when you use a comma to separate two main clauses. Two other ways to eliminate comma splice are to use a period or a semicolon to separate the clauses.

> Production companies travel to distant locations, and sometimes they employ local extras.

Using Commas Correctly

Insert commas where necessary in the following sentences.

1. Movies not plays have become the most-talked-about form of mass entertainment.

2. Very young children prefer animated movies with cartoon characters; adults movies with human actors.

3. Just after a recent movie release video stores were mobbed by teenage girls wanting a copy of the film, which featured the latest teen idol.

4. Alex enjoys watching movies about conspiracies and he also enjoys foreign films.

5. The new adventure movie's premiere in Los Angeles was hectic; in other cities much calmer.

6. During the tragic movie sobs filled the theater.

7. Movie buffs unlike casual moviegoers like to memorize all the lines from their favorite movies.

8. For aspiring bands performing on a movie soundtrack is a good way to gain exposure.

9. Films without sound to accompany the action were called silent movies but they were usually played with piano music.

10. In computer-generated movies special effects often appear amazingly realistic and complex.

11. Movies based on a book may follow the storyline of the book exactly or the screenwriters may make alterations.

12. Watching a movie at the movie theater not at home makes filmwatching a real event.

13. To produce their movies, major production studios spend millions of dollars; independent studios much less.

14. Besides those by Shakespeare old plays made into movies are not my favorites.

Lesson 3

Fixing Comma Problems

More Practice

A. Using Commas Correctly

Add commas where necessary in the following sentences. Circle any commas that should be removed.

1. On her red lipstick looks too harsh.
2. Our refrigerator has been delivered but now it must be connected properly.
3. Bryan likes mystery stories; Carla science fiction.
4. Books unlike stories broadcast on television can be picked up or put down at your convenience.
5. Goldilocks found Papa Bear's bed to be too hard; Mama Bear's too soft.
6. *Iron John* was an immensely successful bestseller yet it had been rejected by many publishers, and viewed favorably by only two.
7. The knight continued his quest for it had become an obsession.
8. Listening to a story on the radio unlike seeing one on the television forces you to use your imagination in picturing characters and settings.
9. The *Titanic* was supposed to be unsinkable but it sank on its maiden voyage.
10. Beach vacations not trips to the mountains were his preference.
11. Firefighters and police officers say the authors face increased dangers in today's society.
12. For entertainment Mr. Allen chooses the opera; Mrs. Allen the hockey game.

B. Using the Comma in Paragraphs

Add commas and conjunctions where they are necessary in the following paragraphs. Use a caret ‸ to show where the conjunction should be added.

In the movie industry motion pictures are divided into three types of films. The first two types, feature films and animated films, are usually released first to theaters. The third type, documentary films, are often premiered on television. Feature films and animation films unlike documentaries are usually fiction. Having a prepared soundtrack is often helpful for animators can draw characters that move simultaneously with the sound. Documentaries not feature films are often made on the less expensive 16 mm film. Documentary makers have the option of shooting on location, they can decide to assemble a film from previously recorded materials. Producers ensure that the movie receives financing, they are also responsible for hiring the key players in film production. Directors not producers are responsible for guiding the actors and production crew and for fulfilling the vision of the writers.

Fixing Comma Problems

Lesson 3

Application

A. Proofreading for Comma Usage

Insert this proofreading symbol ⁊ to add commas where they are needed. Cross out any commas that are not necessary. Insert conjunctions using a caret ⁁ as needed to avoid comma splices.

Drama is written, material meant to be performed. Drama is sometimes defined as the written script; theater as the performance. Originally, tragedy and comedy were separate categories of drama, William Shakespeare eventually inserted comedy into his tragedies. Tragedy unlike comedy has a serious tone, and covers profound issues. Tragedies usually end with the death of the main character, comedies end happily. "To delight and to instruct" Roman writer Horace said, was the purpose of a drama. All dramas contain both purposes. Some dramas seem to focus more on entertainment; others on instruction. Drama is a useful means of expression for a society, can use it to reflect on itself and its values and beliefs.

Perhaps early Greek playwrights had the greatest influence on drama. Aristotle divided the elements of drama into plot, character, thought, language, and spectacle; however, he considered the most important element to be plot. Nowadays unlike during the times of ancient Greece the balance of these elements may vary. Many writers prefer to emphasize character to allow actors to reveal their humanity in challenging roles. In that way the play can focus on a particular theme or issue.

B. Writing with Commas

Correct each of these comma splices in three different ways, that is, by splitting the sentence into two sentences, by using a semicolon, and by adding a conjunction. Write your revised sentence or sentences on the line. Draw a star by the revision you like best.

1. Vegetarians can eat a healthy diet, they must plan their diets carefully.

_____

_____

_____

2. The guide was quite knowledgeable, she called our attention to details in the painting.

_____

_____

_____

CHAPTER 9

Lesson 4

Other Comma Rules

Teaching

Use a **comma** in these situations:

- to set off a personal title or a business abbreviation
  Example: Albert Vargo, Jr., is my cousin.
- in the salutation of a personal letter and the closing of any letter
  Example: Dear Uncle Jim,   Your niece,
- between the day of the month and the year, and, in a sentence, after the year
  Example: Carla was born in Chicago on February 17, 1987, and moved here last year.
- to separate the street, city, and state in addresses and names of places (Do not use a comma between the state and the ZIP code)
  Example: I live at 1452 Bellfield Blvd., Columbus, Ohio, in the home my grandfather built.
- in numbers of more than three digits to denote thousands (except calendar years)
  Example: The distance to the sun from Earth is 93,000,000 miles.
- to set off a direct quotation from the rest of the sentence
  Example: The chef said, "This is a culinary masterpiece."

Using Commas Correctly

Insert commas where necessary in the following sentences.

1. Dear Aunt Regina

   My friends and I will be visiting London on October 10, and we were hoping you would have the time to accompany us to the Tower of London.
   Your niece

2. "Lima was founded" the guide told us "at a site called Plaza de Armas in 1535."

3. The site of the Boston Massacre, which occurred on March 5 1770 is a popular tourist spot today.

4. Beijing is a densely populated city with a population of over 11000000 people.

5. Historian Graham Richards Sr. often gives tours of New Orleans in his spare time.

6. The residence of the prime ministers of Great Britain is 10 Downing Street London.

7. St. Petersburg is the home of the Russian Revolution, which took place on October 24 and October 25 1917.

8. "The Taj Mahal" my mother read "was built by Shah Jahan in memory of his wife, who died in 1631."

9. Denver is called the Mile-High City because a spot on the Capitol steps is at 5280 feet above sea level.

10. We left our house at 45 Scarlett Drive Albany New York this morning at 5 A.M.

11. Our class visited the grounds where the Battle of Gettysburg took place on July 1–3 1863 and where President Lincoln gave his address on November 19 1863.

12. By the end of the Battle of Gettysburg, the Union army had lost 23000 men, and the Confederate army had lost 25000 men.

13. An entertaining place to visit is Mann's Chinese Theater on Hollywood Boulevard Los Angeles California, which displays the handprints and footprints of movie stars.

Other Comma Rules

More Practice

A. Using Commas Correctly

Add commas where necessary in the following sentences.

1. I live at 12900 Richland Lane Herndon VA 22071.

2. When she opened the letter, she read the closing, "Your former friend John."

3. On April 30 1789 George Washington was inaugurated.

4. The Consumers Union of U.S. Inc. at 256 Washington St. Mount Vernon NY 10553 researches and evaluates products for readers of its magazine.

5. When did you first learn that light travels at a speed of 186000 miles per second?

6. Address all inquiries to Frothingham Ltd. before May 5 1990.

7. Tom Ross Jr. M.D. has opened an office at 1448 Oak Street Cincinnati Ohio.

8. On average the sun is 93000000 miles from Earth.

9. "I'll send you the package or deliver it myself" Joyce promised.

10. "An area of high pressure will bring us fair weather" the forecaster predicted.

11. World War I ended on November 11 1918, a day that used to be called Armistice Day.

12. What famous event happened on July 20 1969?

13. Dear Aunt Harriet
    Thanks for the binoculars. They will come in handy on my hiking trip.
    Your nephew
    Ted

14. Has the population of Boston Massachusetts risen or fallen over the past decade?

15. "A fool and his money are soon parted" says an old proverb.

B. Using the Comma in Paragraphs

Add commas where they are necessary in the following paragraphs.

Dear Grandma

On August 17 I visited Plimoth Plantation in Plymouth Massachusetts. I learned that in 1620 colonists sailed over 3000 miles from England. Small groups of colonists looked for a good place to settle. On December 21 1620 one group landed in Plymouth. They decided to settle there. The people who work at Plimoth Plantation speak as the colonists did in the 1620s. They say "We wish thee a good morrow." Today we would just say "Good morning."

I have enjoyed this trip, but I can't wait to be back with you in Chicago Illinois.

Your grandson
Russell

CHAPTER 9

Other Comma Rules

Application

A. Proofreading for Comma Usage

Write an original story using at least five of the following phrases and abbreviations. Be sure to use commas correctly in your story.

$1350	1450 Main Street Pleasantville Ohio	July 4 2050
Keith Morelli, Jr.	Dear Aunt Jeanie	He shouted
6865000	Yours truly	Las Vegas Nevada
National Widget Corp.		

_____

_____

_____

_____

_____

_____

_____

_____

B. Writing with Commas

Write a personal narrative about a holiday you have celebrated or one that you imagine you could celebrate in the future. In your narrative, include the following situations where a comma is needed: a personal title, a date, a complete address, a number greater than 999, and a direct quotation.

_____

_____

_____

_____

_____

_____

_____

_____

Lesson 1 # Semicolons and Colons   *Teaching*

Use a **semicolon** in the following ways: to join the independent clauses of a compound sentence if no coordinating conjunction is used; to join clauses of a compound sentence that are joined by a conjunctive adverb or transitional phrase; between independent clauses joined by a conjunction if either clause contains commas, and to separate items in a series if those items contain commas.

> Dance is a natural response to rhythm; people dance in all cultures.
> Dance is not a new art form; in fact, we have evidence that prehistoric peoples danced.
> Cave paintings, such as those found in Africa and southern Europe, show ancient dancers; the dances tell us much about how the people lived.
> People today enjoy such dance forms as ballet, which is more formal; line dancing, which is less formal; and ballroom dancing.

Use a **colon** in the following ways: after an independent clause to introduce a list of items, between two independent clauses when the second clause explains or elaborates on the first, and to introduce a long or formal quotation.

> People dance for the following reasons: to tell a story, to create art, and to have a good time.
> Dancing is also healthy: it tones muscles and provides a good workout.
> Agnes DeMille once said this about dance: "The truest expression of a people is in its dances and its music. . . . Bodies never lie."

Use a colon in these additional ways: after the salutation in a formal business letter (Dear Sirs:); between numerals indicating hours and minutes (6:15); and to separate numerals in references to certain religious works, such as the Bible, the Qur'an (Koran), and the Talmud (Mark 5:2).

Using the Semicolon and Colon

Add semicolons and colons appropriately to the following sentences.

1. Dancing is a way to communicate with others a dance may establish a mood, depict an emotion, or tell a story.

2. As noted in Second Samuel 6 14–16, King David of Israel danced during a special religious occasion.

3. Folk dancing consists of traditional dances of a particular ethnic group in fact, the dancers often wear costumes reflecting their heritage.

4. Classical ballet dancers are highly trained they make difficult bodily movements seem effortless.

5. Every list of influential modern dancers includes the following names Isadora Duncan, Ruth St. Denis, Paul Taylor, and Twyla Tharp.

6. In many traditional Asian dances, small movements and gestures convey the story even a slight facial expression has significant meaning.

7. The square dance caller loudly intoned "Do-si-do, then swing your partner, and promenade."

8. Dances popular in the U.S. at one time include the following the cakewalk, the Charleston, the jitterbug, and the twist.

9. Dear Sir
   Saturday's swing dance will be held at 7 30 in the school gym.
   Sincerely,

Lesson 1   Semicolons and Colons   *More Practice*

A. Using the Semicolon and the Colon

Using the proofreader's marks for a semicolon [;] and a colon [:], indicate the correct punctuation for the following sentences.

1. The Rio Grande is one of the longest rivers in North America it flows for 1,885 miles, from Colorado to the Gulf of Mexico.

2. J. R. Tolkien's trilogy, *The Lord of the Rings,* includes these three books *The Fellowship of the Ring, The Two Towers,* and *The Return of the King.*

3. We should have called before we came it would have been considerate.

4. The sermon focused on a quote from John 2 10.

5. We have finished studying Chaucer and Milton next we will study Shakespeare.

6. Dear Sir or Madam
I am responding to your ad in last Sunday's newspaper.

7. At camp Tracey played baseball, soccer, and basketball but she enjoyed water-skiing the most.

8. I love Mexican, Thai, and Chinese food but Martin likes hot dogs and apple pie.

9. John C. Gardner, Jr., has said of the pursuit of excellence "But excellence implies more than competence. It implies a striving for the highest standards in every phase of life."

10. His e-mail message was short and slightly terse nevertheless, she was happy to know he had reached his destination safely.

11. Our fundraisers have been profitable we have $2,500 in the class treasury.

12. The bus wasn't supposed to come until 12 45!

B. Using the Semicolon and the Colon in Writing

Add semicolons and colons where they are needed in these paragraphs.

    (1) Dancing is one of the oldest forms of self-expression in fact, prehistoric cave paintings dating back 20,000 years include pictures of dancers. **(2)** The ancient Egyptians danced at parades, funerals, and religious ceremonies the festival honoring the god Osiris was one such occasion. **(3)** Dancing also was a form of entertainment royalty and wealthy families watched dance performances with their guests. **(4)** The Greeks considered dancing of utmost importance for these reasons to worship properly, to convey meaning in their drama, and to build skill and self-control in warfare education.

    (5) Ancient Romans imitated many Greek customs they also danced for religious festivals. **(6)** Roman dancers added another element to their performances they juggled and did acrobatics while dancing. **(7)** However, not all Romans approved of dancing. **(8)** Cicero, a well-known orator, is credited as stating "No man dances unless he is drunk or insane."

Semicolons and Colons   *Application*

A. Writing Sentences with Semicolons and Colons

For each item, write the sentence following the instructions in parentheses.

> **EXAMPLE** (Use a semicolon to join the parts of a compound sentence without a coordinating conjunction.)
> *The dancer practiced her steps for weeks; she was determined to perform perfectly.*

1. (Use a semicolon before a conjunctive adverb and a comma to join clauses in a compound sentence.)

_____

_____

2. (Use a colon to introduce a long quotation.)

_____

_____

3. (Use a colon to introduce a list of items.)

_____

_____

4. (Use a semicolon to separate parts when commas appear within parts of a series.)

_____

_____

B. Proofreading a News Article

Add necessary semicolons and colons to these paragraphs.

Picture Americans gliding, hopping, shaking, or strutting on the dance floor social dancing has undergone many changes in the last 100 years or so. At the beginning of the 20th century, the popular dance was the cakewalk a couple would execute intricate footwork while high-stepping to syncopated music. In 1912, ballroom dancers Vernon and Irene Castle introduced Latin American rhythms to America the tango, with its dramatic shifts between slow and quick steps, was quite a hit. The 1920s brought a new dance routine waving their arms and kicking their legs, "flappers" enjoyed doing the Charleston. The next dance rage was the jitterbug highly energetic couples danced to the music of the 1930s and 1940s swing bands.

In the 1950s, rock and roll brought these changes in social dancing the couples danced without touching each other, the dancers made up their steps, and the style was freer. Disco dancing was popular in the 1970s and in a complete reversal, couples once again followed certain steps while holding each other. The 1980s and 1990s saw the rise of line dances the electric slide and the macarena are two examples. As for the future, an anonymous dancer has been quoted as saying "New music inspires new dances. Check with me at 12 00 A.M. next year and I'll demonstrate the newest steps."

Lesson 2

Hyphens, Dashes, and Ellipses

Teaching

Hyphens Use a hyphen in the following places:

- when part of a word must be carried over from one line to the next (Words should be divided between syllables. Keep at least two letters together on a line. When in doubt about syllabification, consult a dictionary.)
- in compound numbers from twenty-one to ninety-nine, and in fractions, such as two-thirds
- in certain compound nouns, such as *sister-in-law, great-grandfather*
- in compound adjectives used before (but not after) a noun, such as *well-known*
- in words with the prefixes *ex-,* or *quasi-,* and with the suffix *-elect.* (Do not use a hyphen with *pre-, pro-,* or *re-*)
- to avoid confusion or to avoid repeating a vowel or consonant, for example, *pre-exist, bell-like*

Dashes Use dashes for the following reasons:

- to set off explanatory, supplementary, or parenthetical material in sentences. *Example:* Madrigals—songs popular during the 16th century—are still fun to sing.

Ellipses Remember the following guidelines for using ellipses.

- Use three ellipsis points (three spaced periods preceded and followed by spaces) to show that one or more words have been omitted within a quoted sentence. *Example:* "The critics are raving about . . . this film."
- Use a period and three ellipsis points if the ellipses fall at the end of a sentence. *Example:* "The band's rise has been phenomenal. . . ."
- In fiction and informal writing, ellipses are used to indicate that an idea has trailed off. *Example:* Somehow I felt disappointed; I felt . . .

A. Using Hyphens and Dashes

Using the proofreader's marks for a hyphen [=] and a dash [$\frac{1}{m}$], insert correct punctuation as needed.

1. A little known assistant replaced the ailing conductor for the matinee performance.
2. Popular music country, jazz, rock, and folk is played on threefourths of our local stations.
3. The well liked guitarist played three encores.
4. Mr. McGreavy a selfemployed piano tuner worked on the concert grand piano.
5. Igor Stravinsky a modern Russian composer rejected preexisting forms of music to forge his own style.

B. Using Ellipses

Read the passage and then compare it with the numbered quotes below. Circle the number of the quote that uses ellipses correctly.

> The mockingbird had ceased to sing. The leaves of the bougainvillaea vine which clambered over the dining-room wall rustled faintly. Mrs. Delahanty began taking the spoons from the serving dishes.
>
> —Jessamyn West, "Mr. Cornelius, I Love You"

1. The mockingbird had ceased to sing. The leaves of the bougainvillaea vine . . . rustled faintly. Mrs. Delahanty began taking the spoons from the serving dishes.
2. The mockingbird had ceased to sing. . . .The leaves of the bougainvillaea vine which clambered over the dining-room wall rustled . . .

Lesson 2 — Hyphens, Dashes, and Ellipses   *More Practice*

A. Using the Hyphen

In these sentences, underline each word that requires a hyphen and write the corrected word on the line at the right.

1. Grades one through five are usually taught in
   selfcontained classrooms.   _____

2. The Mayorelect will take over the job on January 17.   _____

3. Relax. You just have preelection jitters.   _____

4. Just imagine having your motherinlaw be the President of the
   United States.   _____

5. According to the survey, eightysix percent of the citizens
   approve of recycling.   _____

B. Using Dashes in Sentences

Rewrite each sentence, inserting dashes where they are needed.

1. Rock and roll a type of music born in the 20th century is a respected art form.

   _____

2. This was the first okay, the second time that I played that CD at high volume.

   _____

3. When I was in high school about 100 years ago I was in a band, too.

   _____

4. Our band if I remember correctly was fairly popular for a while.

   _____

C. Using Ellipses

Read the following passage. Then choose the passage below in which ellipses points have been used correctly to quote the passage. Circle the number of that passage.

> Soon the men began to gather, surveying their own children, speaking of planting and rain, tractors and taxes. They stood together, away from the pile of stones in the corner, and their jokes were quiet and they smiled rather than laughed.
> —Shirley Jackson, "The Lottery"

1. Soon the men began to gather, surveying their own children, speaking of planting and rain, tractors and taxes. They stood together, away from the pile of stones in the corner, and their jokes were quiet. . . .

2. Soon the men began to gather, surveying their. . . . tractors and taxes. They stood together, ... and they smiled rather than laughed.

⬤ Lesson 2 Hyphens, Dashes, and Ellipses

Application

A. Proofreading for Correct Punctuation

Indicate where hyphens or dashes are needed in the following paragraph.

> **EXAMPLE** It is widely believed that the guitar is the best-known stringed instrument. Violinists—and I'm one of them—probably would dispute that.

Ethereal, belllike tunes are the distinguishing mark of one of the oldest stringed instruments the harp. Early types of the harp the greatgrandparents, so to speak have been found in many ancient civilizations in the Near East. In the 700s, the first harps appeared in Ireland the Irish harp is still the national symbol and soon became wellknown throughout Europe. Today, harps large concert versions or smaller ones are found anywhere from world renowned orchestras to local folk bands.

The best known harp the modern concert instrument is large and imposing. It rests on a *pedestal* (base), while the *pillar*, the *neck*, and the *soundbox* the part that rests on the harpist's shoulder form the sides of this triangularlyshaped instrument. Between the neck and the soundbox are 47 strings, which can be set over a range of six and onehalf octaves. Seven pedals these extend from the pedestal can be utilized to raise or lower the pitch of the strings.

The harpist plucks the strings only the thumb and first three fingers of each hand are used and depresses the pedals with his or her feet. The harp is a challenging instrument for both the semiserious student and the accomplished musician.

B. Using Ellipses

Write a conversation between two people who meet at a concert or dance, but have almost nothing in common. Use ellipses to show how sentences trail off and how long pauses develop when speakers can't think of what to say next.

_____

_____

_____

_____

_____

_____

_____

_____

_____

_____

_____

Apostrophes   *Teaching*

Follow these guidelines when using apostrophes to form possessives:

- For a singular noun, an indefinite pronoun, or a compound indefinite pronoun, add an apostrophe and an *s*, as in *one player's helmet*, *somebody's key*, and *no one else's fault*. To form the possessive of certain classical or Biblical names that end in *s*, simply add an apostrophe, for example, *Achilles'*.

- For a plural noun that ends in *s* or *es*, add only an apostrophe after the final *s*, for example, *two players' helmets*.

- For a plural noun that does not end in *s*, add an apostrophe and an *s*, for example, *people's opinions*.

- For a compound noun, add an apostrophe and an *s* to only the last part of the noun, for example, *president-elect's reception*.

- If the names of two or more persons are used to show joint ownership, add an apostrophe and an *s* only to the last name, for example, *Grant and Phil's project*.

- If the names of two or more persons are used to show individual possession, add an apostrophe and an *s* to both names, for example, *Grant's and Phil's eyes*.

Other uses of apostrophes include the following:

- Use an apostrophe to show the omission of letters in contractions, for example, *it's* = *it is;* digits in a year number, for example, *'54* (but not in decades or centuries, as in 1600s); or sounds in poetry or in dialects, for example *o'er*.

- Use an apostrophe to form the plurals of letters, numerals, abbreviations containing periods, and words used as words, for example, *A's, 10's, M.D.'s, no's.*

- Add an apostrophe to the possessive forms of nouns expressing measures of time or amount when they are used as adjectives, for example, *two cents' worth, one day's time*.

Using the Apostrophe

On the line at the right, write the possessive form of the boldfaced word or words or the contraction that can be made from the two words boldfaced in each sentence.

1. **Roger** and **Diane** Siamese cat ran away while they were on vacation.   _____

2. **Everyone** vote really counts in this election.   _____

3. We **can not** be certain of victory at this point in the campaign.   _____

4. Two **players** names were placed on the injured list.   _____

5. Is either of the two **brothers-in-law** time free this Saturday? _____

6. **Janine** and **Tanisha** winter coats both have fake fur collars. _____

7. **Jesus** Sermon on the Mount was recorded by at least one of his apostles.   _____

8. **It has** been a long time since we saw each other last.   _____

Name _____ Date _____

Apostrophes

More Practice

A. Using the Apostrophe

Underline any words that need apostrophes or apostrophes and *s*'s in the following sentences. Then, in the space on the right, write the word correctly.

1. Lakisha report card was filled with *A*s and *B*s.   _____

2. Whether the bus will arrive on time is anyone guess.   _____

3. Ulysses journeys encompassed many strange and terrifying adventures.   _____

4. Several band members instruments were damaged when the band
   room flooded.   _____

5. The choir visited the children ward at the hospital.   _____

6. Jason found his sister-in-law picture in the 92 yearbook.   _____

7. Claudia and Laura duet won second prize in the music contest.   _____

8. Twelve students received their Ph.D.s in biology at the graduation
   ceremony.   _____

9. Loud yes and no filled the air as the spectators listened to the
   political debate.   _____

10. Can you imagine how many changes you'll make in one year time?   _____

11. Anthony and Bridget speeches electrified the crowd.   _____

12. Both teams coaches disputed the call.   _____

13. Fernando dog was so muddy he couldnt recognize it.   _____

B. Using the Apostrophe Correctly

Rewrite each sentence, adding apostrophes where necessary.

1. The public doesnt always recognize geniuses in its midst.

   _____

2. Youre invited to a holiday party at Fran and Erics house this Saturday.

   _____

3. Socrates unorthodox opinions caused some people to distrust him.

   _____

4. Cant you give one hours worth of time for a good cause?

   _____

5. The childrens and adults book collections are housed in different rooms in
   this library.

   _____

CHAPTER 10

Apostrophes

Application

A. Proofreading for Correct Punctuation

In the following paragraph, look for words in each sentence that require apostrophes or apostrophes and *s*'s. First, underline them, and then write those words correctly on the corresponding lines below. If no words in a sentence require changes, write **Correct** on the line.

      (1) Out of nature abundant resources comes a product with thousands of uses. **(2)** Composed chiefly of sand, soda, and lime, glass is used in everything from skyscrapers windows to a mother-in-law spectacles. **(3)** Foods, liquids, and medicines are contained in glass for safety's sake. **(4)** Scientists laboratories are filled with beakers, test tubes, and other glass equipment. **(5)** Mom and Dad kitchen has its share of glass tumblers and cookware. **(6)** Special heat-resistant clothing, such as that for firefighters and astronauts suits, is made from fiberglass. **(7)** Drivers are safer because of the laminated glass in their windshields. **(8)** Works of art made of glass are formed by men and women skilled hands. **(9)** Depending on its use, glass can be made to imitate Hercules strength or a spiderweb fragility. **(10)** If asked, one wouldnt be hard-pressed to recite several uses of glass in a minutes time.

1. _____   6. _____

2. _____   7. _____

3. _____   8. _____

4. _____   9. _____

5. _____   10. _____

B. Writing with Correct Punctuation

Follow the directions to write and punctuate sentences correctly.

1. Write a sentence that uses an apostrophe to show possession in a plural noun ending in *s*.

_____

2. Write a sentence that uses an apostrophe to show possession in a singular noun.

_____

3. Write a sentence that discusses joint possession by two people and uses apostrophes appropriately.

_____

4. Write a sentence that discusses individual possession by two people and uses apostrophes appropriately.

_____

Quotation Marks and Italics *Teaching*

Lesson 4

Use **quotation marks** (" ") at the beginning and at the end of a direct quotation. Do not use quotation marks to set off an indirect quotation. Punctuate a speaker's words with a period, comma, question mark, or exclamation point inside quotation marks. Use a comma to replace an ending period before words such as *he said*. Enclose both parts of a divided quotation in quotation marks. Do not capitalize the first word of the second part unless it begins a new sentence.

> Bethany asked, "Are you familiar with any proverbs from other countries?"
> "If you page through *Bartlett's Familiar Quotations*," replied Ben, "you'll note that many nations have wise sayings."

Put colons or semicolons outside the closing quotation mark.

> Many proverbs are found in "compendiums"; that is, brief but complete listings of an extensive subject.

Use single quotation marks when you write a quotation within another quotation.

> "I like a Japanese proverb which states, 'Life is for one generation; a good name is forever,'" said May.

If the quotation consists of more than one paragraph, begin each paragraph with a quotation mark; do not use a closing quotation mark until the end of the entire quotation.

Use quotation marks to enclose the titles of magazine articles, chapters, short stories, TV episodes, essays, and poems or songs. Use them to enclose slang words, unusual expressions, technical terms, and definitions of words.

Use **italics** for titles of long works and for names of vehicles. Also, italicize unfamiliar foreign words, phrases, or words referred to as words. When writing by hand or using a typewriter, use underlining to indicate italics.

A. Writing Sentences with Quotation Marks and Italics

Add quotation marks, commas, and end marks where necessary in each sentence. Also underline any word that should be italicized. If the sentence is correct, write **Correct** on the line.

1. Jury duty, said the speaker, is both a privilege and an obligation. _____

2. I stayed only three weeks in Hawaii, Mia reported, but I felt at home there. _____

3. My friends told me when I left, "You are now a Kamaaina." Kamaaina means old timer. _____

4. The headline on this old newspaper reads, Dewey Elected President, Latonya said. _____

5. The hall monitor asked me if I had a pass. _____

6. "How can both flammable and inflammable mean the same thing?" asked Anne. _____

Quotation Marks and Italics   *More Practice*

A. Using Quotation Marks

Add quotation marks, commas, and end marks where necessary in each sentence or conversation. Underline any word that should be italicized. One sentence is correct as is.

1. Kayla remarked, There is an old Chinese proverb which states It is not the knowing that is difficult, but the doing.

2. I've often imagined sailing into Boston Harbor on the U.S.S. Constitution mused Patrick.

3. The speaker told us to examine an issue thoroughly before making any judgment.

4. Does anyone know the definitions of the words quasar and quark queried Ms. Stanley?

5. There is an interesting article in Nature Magazine declared Maurice. It's about the discovery of an intact woolly mammoth in Siberia.

6. One of my favorite poems is To Helen; it was written by Edgar Allan Poe.

7. Would actuate or activate be the better word to use in this sentence? asked Carl.

8. What a great way to publicize our fundraiser exclaimed Rita.

9. I enjoyed the irreverent humor in Mark Twain's book The Innocents Abroad Brian stated.

10. "The mid-19th century saw the rise of a special group of writers. Totally American in their outlook and unafraid to experiment, they took on new themes and ideas.

   Writers such as Twain and Hawthorn related the American experience and celebrated the American people. Poets such as Whitman and Dickinson experimented with new forms of verse. These and other writers created a unique American literature recognized throughout the world."

B. Using Quotation Marks in a Dialogue

Add quotation marks, commas, and end marks where necessary. Underline any words that should be italicized.

   While Ann and I were doing research on our term paper, began Susan, we discovered an interesting remark by Oliver Wendell Holmes in a book called Over the Teacups.
   Ann continued, Holmes stated When you write in prose you say what you mean. When you write in rhyme you say what you must.
   Do you think other writers felt this way, too? asked Susan.
   Robert noted, Emerson presented his philosophy in essays, such as Self-Reliance, and in his poetry as well."
   Yes, but I think Holmes meant something deeper, persisted Susan. Does anyone dig what I'm saying?
   Everyone began to giggle uncontrollably.
   I guess we'll continue our discussion another time, sighed Susan.

Lesson 4

Quotation Marks and Italics

Application

A. Correcting Misuse of Quotation Marks and Italics

Rewrite the following sentences, using quotation marks, commas, and end marks correctly. In your rewritten sentence, underline any words that should be italicized.

1. "Wow" "What an experience I had last evening"! exclaimed Teresa. Our family had tickets to the New York Ballet's performance of Swan Lake."

_____

_____

2. "I saw the review in the "Daily Register" this morning, said Dylan. The reviewer said, "The performance was outstanding and ballerina Lucinda Lopez was brilliant."

_____

_____

3. "Not only did we see the ballet", Teresa remarked, but we also met Lucinda afterward, and she autographed my copy of the article Notable American Ballerinas."

_____

_____

4. Felicia chimed in, "According to an article in Ballet Magazine, she's a "rising star;" everyone expects great things of her.

_____

_____

5. "No more complaining about practicing the jeté and entrechat, declared Teresa. Who knows where it may lead me?"

_____

_____

B. Writing with Quotation Marks

Write a dialogue in which two students discuss their plans after high school graduation. Make sure that you indicate clearly who is speaking. Use quotation marks and other punctuation marks correctly. Include one word, phrase, or title that should be italicized.

_____

_____

_____

_____

_____

Parentheses and Brackets   *Teaching*

Use **parentheses** ( ) to enclose supplemental or explanatory material added to a sentence. When parenthetical material occurs within a sentence, do not capitalize the first word or end with a period. You may end with a question mark or exclamation point.

> The Mammoth-Flint Ridge cave system extends at least 190 miles (306 kilometers).
> Many caves (have you ever been to Mammoth Cave?) are tourist attractions.

Put punctuation marks after the closing parenthesis, not before the opening parenthesis.

Punctuate and capitalize a parenthetical sentence that stands by itself as you normally would.

> Some sports enthusiasts enjoy cave exploration even though it can be dangerous. (Can you imagine being stuck in a dark, cold cave?)

Use parentheses to identify a source of information, to enclose figures or letters that identify items in a series, and to set off numerical information such as area codes.

> Most caves are formed in limestone or in a related rock, such as marble or dolomite. *(World Book Encyclopedia)*
> Caves fascinate me for three reasons: (1) their mystery, (2) their beauty, and (3) their danger.

Use **brackets** [ ] to enclose additions or explanation within quoted material or to enclose parenthetical material that appears within parentheses.

> One cave explorer says, "That passage [in Carlsbad Caverns] gets awfully narrow at spots."
> Mammoth Cave National Park is a favorite destination for families on vacation. (The Web site for the national parks is useful for planning a visit [see http://www.nps.gov].)

A. Using Parentheses

Place parentheses where they are needed in the following sentences.

1. "Large numbers of bats roost in caves during the day and fly out at night to hunt for insects." *World Book Encyclopedia*

2. *Troglodytes* blind, colorless animals living deep in caves include the following species: 1 beetles, 2 fish, and 3 spiders.

3. The Giant's Hall in Luray Caverns have you seen it? contains breath-taking rock formations of enormous proportions.

4. The ceiling of Waitomo Cave in New Zealand is covered with glowworms those funny creatures

B. Using Brackets

Place brackets to follow the directions (in italics) for each sentence.

1. Edgar Allan Poe wrote: "This maiden Annabel Lee lived with no other thought than to love and be loved by me." Indicate *that* this maiden *refers to Annabel Lee.*

2. "That novel *To Kill a Mockingbird* introduced me to unforgettable characters," said Dolores. Indicate *that* That novel *refers to* To Kill a Mockingbird.

3. The canyon's trails are well marked and rated as appropriate for beginners. All park trails are rated in my new book. See page 25. Indicate that the reader will find a list of trail ratings in the writer's book on page 25.

Parentheses and Brackets

More Practice

Using Parentheses and Brackets

Rewrite each sentence using parentheses, brackets, or both.

1. Spelunkers cave explorers should carry these pieces of equipment: 1 sturdy ropes or cables, 2 a hard hat, and 3 two light sources—a headlamp and a flashlight.

_____

_____

2. Spelunkers must have no fear of enclosed spaces. That requirement, I must admit, makes the sport off-limits for me.

_____

_____

3. "I think that the first people to discover this huge and impressive cave Mammoth Cave must have been awestruck by its size," said the naturalist.

_____

_____

4. The *Handbook for Spelunking* reminds cave enthusiasts that "the cave environment is fragile, and speleothems mineral deposits that hang from the ceiling or rise from the floor can be destroyed easily."

_____

_____

_____

5. "The best-known kinds of speleothems are stalactites and stalagmites." *World Book Encyclopedia*

_____

_____

6. Many of the world's caves have vast areas that remained undiscovered and unexplored. (A complete listing of the extent of explored caves has recently become available. See Appendix B.)

_____

_____

7. Cavefish fish who spend their entire lives in caves appear pale pink. You're really looking at their blood since their skin is transparent and they have no eyes a pretty image, isn't it?

_____

_____

Parentheses and Brackets   *Application*

A. Using Parentheses and Brackets

Rewrite each sentence by adding or replacing parentheses or brackets.

1. Tonight at the Museum of Natural History a noted speleologist is lecturing on Carlsbad Caverns. For further information, contact the Museum (Call 1-800-NATURAL.)

_____

_____

2. Unusual speleothems found in caves include the following: 1 drapery, 2 flowstone, and 3 helictites.

_____

_____

3. As we entered the chamber, the guide warned, "Please do not touch this formation (a large stalactite) as it is easily broken."

_____

_____

4. Since the cave consisted of only four chambers, the lost hiker a novice spelunker was found within 24 hours. What a relief to his family!

_____

_____

B. Writing with Parentheses and Brackets

Write a sentence using each of these parenthetical expressions. Use the expression either within the sentence or standing by itself. Use brackets at least once.

would you try that?   See page 15   I'd like to try
a good teacher   dates to remember   an unexpected pleasure

_____

_____

_____

_____

_____

_____